THE
MAXIMUM
SECURITY
BOOK CLUB

THE
MAXIMUM
SECURITY
BOOK CLUB

READING LITERATURE

IN A MEN'S PRISON

MIKITA BROTTMAN

HARPER

An Imprint of HarperCollinsPublishers

HarperCollins books may be purchased for educational, business, or sales promotional use. For information, please e-mail the Special Markets Department at SPsales@harpercollins.com.

FIRST EDITION

An extension of this copyright appears on page 231.

Designed by Jo Anne Metsch

Library of Congress Cataloging-in-Publication Data has been applied for.

ISBN: 978-0-06-238433-1

16 17 18 19 20   OV/RRD   10 9 8 7 6 5 4 3 2 1

A12006 826754

It was written I should be loyal to the nightmare of my choice.

—*Heart of Darkness* (Joseph Conrad, 1899)

CONTENTS

INTRODUCTION

For the last three years, I've been running a book club at a men's prison. I started volunteering at the prison as a sabbatical project, but it's become a long-term commitment. My fascination with this place and the men who inhabit it isn't a new impulse; I've long been preoccupied with the lives of people generally considered unworthy of sympathy, especially those who've committed crimes with irreversible moral implications, like murder. Such people, more so even than the rest of us, are unable to escape the past.

Right or wrong, it's to the past that we look when seeking explanations for human behavior, digging through family histories to find motives for present tendencies. So here is mine, in a nutshell. I was born in Sheffield, an industrial city in the north of England, to rebellious young parents with little respect for the law. It was the middle sixties. My father had a Beatle haircut and wore John Lennon glasses; my mother had three children by the time she was twenty-two. On the ceiling above their bed was a purple sticker that said, "Make Love Not War." They believed that if you didn't embrace the values of "mainstream society," the system was stacked against you, and you had to fight it any way you could. They seemed to have no sense of belonging to a broader world and none of the personal authority or autonomy this belonging normally brings. Instead, they saw themselves as victims of the state.

My parents began their adult lives as schoolteachers, though neither, in the end, was cut out for the role. My father stuck with it for more than twenty years, in the meantime fighting "the system" through minor scams (dodging the entrance fees to parks and campgrounds by lifting us over the back fence, or hiding us in the trunk of the car) that were so much a part of our daily life I never questioned them. My mother's style of battle was different. She became radicalized and enlightened, got divorced, stopped cooking our meals, gave up her teaching job, and joined the local Communist Party. She decided my brothers and I no longer needed adult supervision. My brothers stopped going to school and started getting into trouble. They knew they could get away with it; our mother regarded social workers, anxious parents, and the police as "squares" who were against freedom and hung up about sex—selfish, narrow-minded types who only cared about the values of "the Man" (as opposed to loving, freethinking, broad-minded people like us).

By the time I was sixteen, my two brothers had both moved out and gone on the dole. In Sheffield in the 1980s, it was perfectly normal to live on state benefits; everyone did it. I hardly knew anyone with a job. My brothers lived with friends who played in bands, smoked pot, and made their homes in squats or state-subsidized housing. My younger brother became addicted to heroin and spent a brief time in prison on pretrial detention for drug possession charges.

Once both brothers had left home, my mother rented out their bedrooms to hard-luck cases she met in the pub: feckless single mothers, addicts, and ex-cons who shared our bathroom, kitchen, and television room. When she took in a pedophile on the run from the law, I stopped going downstairs at all and retreated to my attic bedroom, where it was so cold I could see my breath. (Whenever I complained, I was asked, "Why don't you put on another sweater?") I closed the curtains, huddled by the electric radiator with my cat, and escaped into books—a habit fostered not by my teachers, I should add, but in spite of them: the government body that eventually closed down my school described it as one of the worst in Britain. ("Poverty invades the school like water flooding a ship," concluded one investigator.)

All that time spent reading paid off: I won a scholarship to study literature at Oxford. Everyone let me know I'd sold out, betrayed my roots. My father warned I'd soon become "posh" and "pretentious." My mother said Oxford was "a bastion of elitism" and I'd be joining "the system." But bad blood runs deep. I didn't realize it at the time, but I'd already absorbed my family's underdog, outlaw mentality.

As a result, I don't think of people in prison as "bad people" who've broken the rules of the "good people" on the outside. Rather, I often think how easily I—how anyone—could end up there. I was lucky enough not to be born to abusive, drug-addicted parents; lucky to be born with a good mind, to be given education and health care and decent food. Of course, not all those people who end up in prison are raised in poverty. Even the most stable and prosperous life can be derailed by an impulsive move with tragic consequences (shooting an intruder, punching a girlfriend, knocking over a pedestrian). Plus, many people in prison claim they are innocent. Why should I disbelieve them? What separates me from these unfortunate souls except my own good fortune? My good fortune so far, I should say; I could still end up behind bars.

Let me add, in case you get the wrong impression of me, that I'm a quiet, private, law-abiding type with no criminal record. I've worked hard to build myself the kind of life I find comfortable, but I've also been incredibly lucky. I've had all kinds of opportunities that haven't come to others, including a world-class, state-financed graduate-level education. To put it simply, I can't help but feel a powerful allegiance to those whose lives haven't worked out so well, and it's partly this feeling that drives me to volunteer at the prison, where I work with the same kinds of people I used to hide from when my mother took them in. Sometimes I worry the compulsion that draws me to these men is less an allegiance than a stranglehold, a form of survivor's guilt that, with enough time and therapy, I'll learn to shake off. Most of the time, however, it feels like an incalculable privilege.

The protagonist of *Heart of Darkness* by Joseph Conrad, a man named Charlie Marlow, is obsessed by the Congo River, which led into what at the time was unmapped territory. "It fascinated me as a snake would a bird," says Marlow. One of the reasons *Heart of Darkness* speaks to me so deeply is because, like Marlow, I, too, am fascinated by dark places and their inhabitants. I think of this tendency as a kind of epistemophilia—the compulsion to find out, to unravel secrets, to question the strictures and conventions of knowledge. I like to turn things over and see what they look like underneath. And in the prison, as the line from Heraclitus has it, "here, too, the gods are present."

*

Jessup Correctional Institution (JCI) was originally constructed as an annex to the huge Maryland House of Correction (better known as "the Cut," after the path forged through a nearby hill during the construction of the Baltimore and Ohio Railroad), a handsome but sinister-looking structure built in 1878 from local brick and stone. Now dismantled, the Cut was notorious for its harsh living conditions, violence among convicts, and frequent assaults on the guards. Most of the men currently incarcerated in JCI arrived there from other prisons, including both the Cut and the Maryland Penitentiary in downtown Baltimore, and they've often entertained me with tales of their past lives in these legendary establishments. When the Cut closed down in 2007, most of its inhabitants were moved to North Branch Correctional Institution in Cumberland, Maryland, a new supermax facility, and JCI went from being an annex to the Cut to becoming a prison in its own right.

To get there, I drive south from Baltimore on Interstate 95, take exit 41, and enter a semirural no-man's-land dotted with administration buildings, truck stops, landfills, and industrial warehouses. These structures are separated by what looks from the highway like pleasant woodland but is in fact a dumping ground for unwanted electrical equipment and rusting industrial trash, as I discovered when I went exploring with my dog. While Grisby was sniffing through piles of abandoned clothing, I was politely asked to leave by a uniformed contractor who told me I was inadvertently trespassing on state property.

Arriving at JCI, I park next to one of the dark blue prison vehicles, which bear Maryland's coat of arms and the motto *Fatti maschii parole femine* ("Manly deeds, womanly words"). I walk over to the front gate and show the correctional officer (CO) my paperwork and ID. If everything's in order, I pass on to the next obstacle: the metal detector. As in a fairy-tale trial, you're given three chances to pass through. I've learned not to wear jewelry, copper hair-clips, or a buckled belt. I take off my watch and ring; then there's always a moment of panic: Did I remember to wear my "prison bra"—the one that's not underwired?

Once the metal detector has given me the all clear, the CO gives me a full-body pat down and I turn in my driver's license in exchange for a pink clip-on visitor's badge. Next, I'm sent to wait by a glass sally port (a double set of mechanically operated steel doors) for a uniformed escort. There's a wooden counter beside me and a handwritten sign on the wall above that says, "Ammunition Loading/Unloading Area."

This is usually the most frustrating part of the entire process. At times, I've had to wait thirty minutes or more for a CO to walk from the school to fetch me, a distance of no more than five hundred yards, which means that although I always arrive at the prison early, I might still be late to meet the prisoners. As I stand waiting, COs will come up to the stand beside me and load or unload their weapons, depending on whether they're coming in or going out (the process makes a metallic clipping sound, like a paper hole puncher). Many are cordial and friendly; some are taciturn; a few seem to be deliberately unhelpful, making it difficult for me to avoid the conclusion that I'm being held up on purpose. I'm unable to contact the prisoners to let them know I'll be late, but they're never annoyed or impatient. However late I arrive, there they are, waiting for me. Where else do they have to go?

According to hiring advertisements, the position of a correctional officer in Maryland requires "the ability to read a limited number of two- and three-syllable words and to recognize similarities and differences between words and numbers," "the ability to add and subtract two-digit numbers, to multiply and divide with 10's and 100's," and "the ability to perform these operations using units of American money and weight measurement, volume, and distance" (this last clause underscores the fact that many COs are African immigrants, mostly from Nigeria). For a job requiring minimal qualifications, the pay isn't bad—around $20 an hour, or $42,000 a year—but it never gets higher than around $55,000, and the position usually involves some overtime. What's more, prison officers have to deal with constant physical threats and face daily hostility from the convicts. Escorting volunteers in and out of the prison must impose additional stress on this heavy workload, and if the COs resent interlopers like me, perhaps they have good reason.

My escort and I next pass through the sally port, up a ramp that leads past the visiting room, and through another door that has to be buzzed open by an officer in a control booth. We exit through a covered walkway, enter the administration building, walk down another hallway, and pass through a second sally port. Here, I sign my name in a book, get the nod from an officer in a glass booth, and enter a concrete yard enclosed on both sides by two sixteen-foot chain-link fences. Neat coils of razor wire roll along the top and fill the gap between. We walk through the compound, past the gun towers, cellblock buildings, and exercise yard with ranks of bleachers, basketball hoops, and a running track. Trapped atop the razor wire is a permanent display of semi-deflated soccer balls. In the warmer weather, sparrows flit busily up and down, building their nests in the fences, and a resident flock of geese amble through the yard.

Finally, we enter the double doors of a one-story cinder-block building into a corridor whose walls are painted with a brightly colored mural depicting religious themes. On the left is a door to the gym, and on the right is the library and the school, which consists of two hallways, six classrooms, a handful of offices, and a room designated as the chapel. A principal and a couple of teachers are employed here full-time to teach basic literacy and GED classes. Beside the principal's office is a bulletin board displaying photographs of prisoner graduation ceremonies and certificates of achievement. These images, like the prisoner-painted murals in the hall, aren't necessarily evidence that creative work is encouraged in the prison, or that JCI is a place of intellectual inspiration; but, like the uplifting stories in the prison newsletter, they show that at least a few of the men who live here do so on equable terms with the authorities.

In 1994, Congress eliminated Pell grants for prisoners, effectively eliminating all college programs in U.S. prisons, including the one at JCI.* I'm one of a small group of volunteers who continue to teach courses to incarcerated men at the college level (though not for college credit). Vincent, a trusted convict with a high level of responsibility, oversees the college program. JCI has no system of orderlies, but Vincent's position is a close equivalent. A slight, young-looking man of fifty-three with a closely trimmed beard, he has a quiet, casual dignity and speaks with intelligence and authority. Over his thirty-plus years in prison, Vincent has earned his GED, and, through the kind of penitentiary extension programs that used to be common, an undergraduate degree in political science and sociology and an MA in humanities. From his cluttered desk in the school office, Vincent negotiates expertly and discreetly between the college program, the principal, the prisoners, and the librarian. It was Vincent

---

* In July 2015, the Obama administration announced that it was planning to reinstate a pilot Pell grant program to a limited number of prisoners seeking college degrees.

VINCENT

who helped me put the book club together once I got my foot in the door, enlisting a group of respectful and literate prisoners, ensuring an appropriate racial balance, and negotiating personality conflicts. I made it clear to him that I wanted discussions in the group to be friendly and as open as possible, given the circumstances; that I wanted everyone to have the chance to speak if they wanted to; and that although we'd be talking about books, we'd also be learning about one another.

Vincent is a member of the book club himself, although his interests are closer to those of the other volunteers who teach in the prison college program, whose classes generally consider broader concerns about race, crime, justice, and similar issues. In fact, virtually all educators who volunteer their time in prisons—and perhaps elsewhere—are based in the humanities and related fields. This is not only because those drawn to these subject areas tend to have a more liberal, idealistic way of thinking—and are seldom paid enough to feel their wisdom is too hard earned to be given away for free—but also because these disciplines require no expensive equipment (unlike, say, classes in engineering, computer science, architecture, or medicine).

My subject is literature. For me, the prison was a new and compelling place for me to talk about books I love with people I wouldn't otherwise get to know. I had no religious or political agenda, no cause to promote, no desire to liberate or enlighten. Nor was I interested in race, crime, power, or the politics of in-carceration, although these subjects, among others, sometimes came up. More so than any of the other professors, I think, my interest in the prisoners was personal.

This wasn't new. I've always taken a personal interest in my students; we often remain close friends. I've never been able to separate my life from my work. I've never wanted to. My writing, research, relationships, and teaching have always been part of the same stream of experience. Imposing boundaries on this kind of life—classifying some relationships as personal and oth-ers professional—has always been impossible for me. But at JCI, boundaries were built into every human encounter, and we were explicitly discouraged from befriending our prison students—we were not allowed, for example, to visit them, write to them, or receive letters or calls from them—which made things difficult, because I found myself increasingly drawn to these men.

Like most academics, I've always favored the brain and tried to deny the body. All my boyfriends have been intellectuals, usu-ally much older than me; when I began volunteering at the prison, my partner, David, and I had been together for almost fifteen years. Our life was a life of books, writing, and talking about ideas. I've never been attracted, as some women are, to muscular quarterback types. In fact, I've always been a little repelled by men with overly defined muscles. I always assume they're going to be arrogant and self-obsessed. Top dogs annoy me: underdogs are more my type.

Getting to know the men in the book club reminded me that this is an incredibly superficial judgment. In Edith Wharton's novel *The House of Mirth*, clever Lily Bart, in search of a husband, is "discerning enough to know that the inner vanity is generally in proportion to the outer self-depreciation." At JCI, I learned the converse is also true: muscles can be a sign of sadness, tattoos can cover lack, and underdogs come in all shapes and sizes. Once I discovered this, the convicts began to fascinate me. At first I was interested in them as case studies, then as suffering human beings, and finally I was curious about them as men. While I didn't necessarily always find them physically attractive, I couldn't help looking at their bodies, just as they couldn't help looking at mine. Beyond this, I found their thoughts and observations compelling, intriguing, and unexpectedly enlightening, and their life stories moving and sad. Toward them, at various times, I felt compassion, sympathy, concern, exasperation, and although I wasn't aware of it at the time, now, looking back, I think I may have even been a little in love.

Although JCI, like all prisons no doubt, is a bleak and depressing place in general, I never mind being in the prison school. In fact, I like the prison classrooms. They have a hermetic, underground feel. Rooms with no external windows are generally considered depressing, but I've always found them particularly snug. While some of the prison classrooms do have external windows, they're too high to see out of, and the vents surrounding the glass dim the daylight. The impression of being underground is enhanced by the absence of clocks, as though the ordinary system of time is in abeyance. There's no Internet access, either, and it's a relief not to have people checking their phones or texting while we talk. I'm not allowed to contact the prisoners outside our time together, nor are they allowed to contact me, so this special place remains sealed off from the outside world. Of course, there are drawbacks to being cut off like this. I can't text David and remind him to feed the cats or let him know what time I'll be home. There are other downsides too. I always crave a decent cup of coffee; I could do without the noise, and—in the warm weather—the smell of food, overflowing toilets, and body odor. But as soon as the discussion begins, all these little irritations disappear.

Before I started the book club, I'd taught a couple of classes in the college program at JCI, one on writing and one on psychology, so by the time we began, in January 2013, I was already growing familiar with the prison and its routine. In some ways, I'd learned, I'm never really alone with the prisoners. A CO always sits at a panel that controls the doors, checking footage from the security cameras that are installed in each room. He also walks up and down the corridor from time to time, glancing through the windows, and sometimes comes in to take the count. If there's ever any tension in the school hallways, it's never between prisoners and volunteers but between prisoners and officers, whose procedures can be humiliating—to the prisoners, that is, not to me. As a woman in a male prison, I've never been pestered or harassed, but then, women in men's prisons aren't as rare as you might think. At JCI the majority of case managers, social workers, nurses, kitchen workers, physical therapists, and COs are women; in fact, bringing female officers into the prison was one of a number of strategic moves to help resolve tension between COs and prisoners. Another was to permit the men to have television sets in their cells. Since the introduction of these two distractions, hostilities have rapidly decreased (although some of the old-timers claim that as soon as television sets were introduced, prisoners rapidly became less politicized and less literate).

After many years teaching literature to university students, I've had plenty of opportunity to learn that, however engaged my students seem to be, I can't kid myself: they're in the class because they need the credits. Whenever I've found myself starting to believe differently, I've tried making attendance optional. Sooner or later I end up facing an empty room. At the prison it's enormously gratifying to be with men who not only want to be there but also tell me my visit is the highlight of their week—and, knowing how the rest of their time is spent, I believe them. At the prison, to use the old comedy punch line, I have a captive audience. The book club always has a long waiting list even though there are no grades, the reading can be difficult and time-consuming, and—since it offers no college credit, has no practical or vocational application, and doesn't focus specifically on rehabilitation—it means less than zero to the parole commission.

In the reading group, I indulge myself by, for the most part, selecting books I love, and our discussions help me to remember why I came to love them in the first place and to think about how I've changed since I first encountered them. Sometimes I share my experiences with the men, and they in turn share their own stories with me. I always try to judge the prisoners as I'd judge anybody else: by my own encounters with them, not by the crimes they might have committed in the past. In doing so, I've found them to be, for the most part, ordinary, decent, kind-hearted men worthy of sympathy and support.

I'm never really sure of my role in the prison, and I often doubt the usefulness of my reading group. I certainly don't see reading as an antidote to unlawful behavior. In books, women who try to use culture to help those worse off than themselves are always deluded. I think of Helen Schlegel in E. M. Forster's *Howards End*, a well-educated, wealthy middle-class woman who tries to help a lower-class man, Leonard Bast, in his quest to enter the realms of "Literature and Art." Her friendship with Bast is misguided and slightly patronizing, since she knows his aesthetic sense is shallow and imitative. He dies when a bookcase falls on him. So much for culture.

I also think of Miss Birdseye in *The Bostonians* by Henry James, a rather ridiculous old lady who's spent her life trying to "emancipate" the poor. "No one had an idea how she lived; whenever money was given her she gave it away to a negro or a refugee . . ." writes James. "Her refugees had been very precious to her; she was always trying to raise money for some cadaverous Pole, to obtain lessons for some shirtless Italian." Miss Birdseye is devoted to the arts, and is always trying to obtain employment for her protégés; yet, the truth is, she has awful taste and hasn't the faintest sense of what makes art or writing powerful.

I can't claim a higher motive, a belief in literature as redemptive, as a way of helping the convicts understand the pain they've brought their victims. On the contrary, I saw the book club mainly as a way for me to share my love for the books that have come to mean the most to me. Still, the motives that drive us are always complex, and we seldom have much insight into our own. It's definitely a boost to my self-esteem to know how important I am to the prisoners, when these days my college students don't even seem to know my name. But I also ask myself: How much does motive really matter? If even the apparently purest act of altruism—the anonymous donation, for example—has some form of payback, whether a private lift to the ego or a more complex unconscious reward, does it make the act itself any less beneficial to the recipient?

I doubt the men in my reading group would think so. These nine prisoners are smart and thoughtful, but they're also tough, hard-edged, and practical. For them, the books we read seem to provide a kind of defensive barrier, as well as a bridge. It's always easier to get to know people when they're not talking about themselves directly, and I soon came to realize that when the men are talking about books, they're also talking about their lives. The book club is a place where they can relax their posturing and defensiveness and, in the guise of discussing literature, talk unguardedly about their memories, the disastrous choices they've made, their guilt, and their remorse. They can bypass the usual ego games and reveal their affections and ambitions, their current and past dilemmas, the defining moments in their lives. In talking about books, they can even broach otherwise taboo subjects such as drug use, homosexuality, and prison power plays. The group brings together men from different housing units, gang affiliations, and racial and religious backgrounds who wouldn't normally spend time together. It's a place and time that permits them to drop their social masks without exposing themselves completely. It's a serious space, but one in which they can still joke, chat, act out, and tease one another (and me).

While I feel great sympathy and fondness for these men, at other times their attitudes bother me. They insist they want to learn and say they're open to new ideas, yet on many subjects they're already rock-solid in their opinions. Surprisingly, given their own predicament, they rarely have sympathy for those like Melville's Bartleby—men they dismiss as losers in the battle of life. These prejudices often strike me as an impediment to understanding. I've always believed that, to remain open to the surprises and contingencies offered by literature, you have to value ignorance more than self-confidence. As a result, I'm rarely fully convinced about anything, always able to see both sides of the argument. I try to stay open to the possibilities of not knowing because, in some ways, I think it's the best frame of mind for reading: every idea, I realize, is open to change. When you believe you know what a book is all about—when a reading becomes fixed and determined—there's no longer room for slippage, for accidents, for the play of the unconscious. The prisoners, however, see my openness as wishy-washy. If this is what you get from literature, they tell me, maybe it's better to leave it alone. Who wants to be uncertain and indecisive? At least they know where they stand.

That may very well be true, I reply, but look where it's got you.

The ten books I chose to read with the prisoners—works by Conrad, Melville, Bukowski, Burroughs, Braly, Shakespeare, Stevenson, Poe, Kafka, and Nabokov—all deal with outsiders who strike out against society, asserting their individuality, right or wrong, against the blind force of "the system" (often the human condition). They're all, in some way or another, subversive books that present familiar situations from a new perspective, letting us see the strangeness in the ordinary and everyday

(a useful skill, you might think, for those trapped in a monotonous daily routine). Most important, they're books that don't
flinch from showing the isolation of the human struggle, the
pain of conflict, and the price that must be paid in consequence—a
price these men know only too well.

At first, I was surprised to find the prisoners' responses to be
so insightful, thought provoking, and articulate. Then I wondered why I'd been expecting any less from them because they've
been in prison for most of their lives, or because they murdered
another human being. Why do we find it so difficult to believe
that men who've killed are as capable of literary appreciation as
anyone else? Is it because we consider them fundamentally lack-
ing in empathy? If a convicted murderer turns out to have a re-
fined literary sensibility, might it suggest that his crime was
caused not by an innate pathology but by the same kind of mo-
mentary bad decision anybody could make? If so, is it merely
accident of circumstance that separates "the murderer" from
"you and me"?

Our group discussions, and my background knowledge,
helped place the books and their authors in a historical and cultural context; but to get a fuller understanding of them, the men
had to read, reflect, and judge on their own, and in private. This
is especially true, I think, of *Heart of Darkness*, a book that, to
some degree at least, is a tale of disconnection from the community. Ironically, if anything in this obscure story is made more
lucid by words, it's our inability to make each other understand
our experiences—as Conrad puts it elsewhere, to make each
other truly *see*. (He also claims that "words, as is well known, are
the great foes of reality.") Marlow isn't much of a storyteller (or
so he claims), and yet he seems somehow compelled to share his
experiences with his listeners—or at least, to make the attempt.

The more deeply he gets involved in his story, however, the more difficult he finds it to express himself. In the end, he begins to realize that we can't share our experiences, coming to the conclusion that "we live as we dream: alone."

Outside prison, the accepted, value-neutral word for an incarcerated individual is "inmate," but within the prison gates, this word is taboo. The men at JCI taught me that in most American prisons, "inmate" is regarded as a euphemism coined by the prison authorities—the equivalent to the average slave of an "Uncle Tom." "The difference between an inmate and a convict," one of the men told me, "is respect." Instead of regarding words like "convict" and "criminal" as demeaning, the prisoners saw them as honest descriptions of their position. In the pages that follow, then, I've adhered to this preference, and avoided the word "inmate."

Jessup Correctional Institution is still officially a maximum security prison. However, its population is no longer made up of lifers with little to lose; in fact, there are only around four hundred lifers remaining. Over the last eight years, the facility has slowly been transitioning to medium security; currently, the prison houses around 1,750 prisoners, of whom around 100 are in the "maximum security" category. The book club contained a number of these men.

I use the term "book club" interchangeably with "reading group," although I realize the two are rather different. While my group was aligned with all the other college-level courses (its official title was Advanced Literature), it was also different and separate from the other classes in the sense that it was limited to nine men, and has continued with the same members (as far as possible) for more than two years. It wasn't a book club in the

usual sense of the term in that I was the person who chose, purchased, and brought in the books, and I also asked the men to
write a one-page weekly response about that week's reading.
Yet, despite the fact that I anchored our discussions by introduc-
ing the books and their authors and occasionally asked questions
or identified passages for discussion, it wasn't a "class" in the
sense that I didn't have anything to "teach" the men. I wanted to
introduce them to some books they wouldn't normally have encountered, and I wanted to hear what they had to say about
them. As it turned out, most of the time I wasn't leading the
group but following, waiting for the chance to rejoin the discussion.

  With two exceptions, I use the names the men are known by
in the prison. In the places where names and small details have
been changed, it's either to maintain the men's safety in the
prison or to uphold the privacy of their victims. Since I wasn't
permitted to record any of our discussions, most of our dialogue
has been reconstituted from memory, my notes made at the
time, the men's written work, and conversations before and after
our meetings. I also read and discussed the manuscript of this
book with the prisoners in the book club, and nothing has been
included without their approval. On May 14, 2015, photographer
Mark Hejnar came into the prison with me to take pictures of
the men. (There are no photographs of either Guy or Kevin, both
of whom left JCI before I began work on this book.) I've also included some sketches made from photographs by illustrator Jess
Bastidas that show the group's changes in membership and seating arrangements. At the request of the Maryland Department
of Public Safety and Correctional Services, I have not shown
photographs of the faces of men who still have living victims. In
the illustrations, these men's faces have been blurred.

Given the many obstacles inherent in any prison environment, it would be unnatural if I did not, from time to time, find myself wondering why I'm giving up my free time to subject myself to the guarded and defensive behavior of the officers. Yet, every time I think about quitting, I realize it's not an option—at least, not yet. The book club is teaching me to see literature in a way I've never seen it before. As often as I've discussed characters like Macbeth, Mr. Kurtz, Bartleby, and Dr. Jekyll—both as a student myself and as a professor—I've never done so with men who actually know what it feels like to kill from ambition, to take pleasure in other people's pain, to look death in the face, to have nothing left to live for. Our conversations may be "only" about literature, but in them everything is at stake.

When I first read these books, I found them tough, because they made me confront difficult subjects: the inevitability of death, our ultimate aloneness, and the absence of any obvious meaning to life. Although they may not have been much fun to read, they helped me explore some very painful subjects, and allowed me to think about hard truths in a serious way. In time, I learned to appreciate the way books like these could lift the veil of subjectivity and, just for a moment, give me a glimpse into moments of other people's existence. They helped me to become attuned to the inner life; they taught me to pay more attention to others, and, as a result, to think more deeply about the different dimensions of individual character and the moral consequences of my own behavior.

This, if anything, is what I hoped the book club would do for the prisoners. I also realized, however, that from their perspective these skills were of little use if they didn't bring the men any nearer to the possibility of release, impress the parole board, or make them more satisfied with their lot. As one man put it to me when I asked why he was leaving the group: "All of what you do is great. However, it will not help me to get out of prison, where I have been for the past twenty-five years." The rewards the book club offered these nine men were intangible and inexpressible, and I never lost sight of the fact that they would surely have preferred to spend their time learning something practical: computer skills, car mechanics, or carpentry, perhaps.

But literature was all I had.

THE
MAXIMUM
SECURITY
BOOK CLUB

1

HEART OF DARKNESS

As an undergraduate at St. Hilda's College, Oxford, I studied English literature. Our first term was devoted to the Victorians. We loved them. We swept happily through the Brontë sisters, Thomas Hardy, Dickens, and even George Eliot ("Jane Austen, but with peasants," as my friend Joanna put it). But our second term was devoted to modernism, and we began with *Heart of Darkness*, which was published in 1899. Here, our ride came to a sad halt.

I tried again and again, but I couldn't seem to get past the first six or seven pages. Reading this difficult novella felt like climbing a slippery cliff: there was nothing to grab on to. Occasionally I thought I'd found a foothold, but the next moment I'd feel myself falling again, unable to focus, losing my place. Everything was "impossible," "impenetrable," "implacable." I'd lie on my bed with the book in my hand, and suddenly I'd be miles away, thinking of a dream I'd had, or wondering what to wear. When-ever I tried to pick up the story's thread again, I'd be lost. In fact, there hardly seemed to be a story at all. It was horribly frustrat-ing. By the day of my tutorial, I'd "got to the end" of the novella only in the sense that I'd looked at the words and turned the pages until there were no more of them to turn.

There was only one scene I could remember, and I could re-member it only because it came early in the story, and I'd found myself reading it over and over again. The protagonist, Marlow, has been hired to replace a steamship captain who's been killed in the Congo after "a scuffle with the natives." Before leaving Europe, Marlow visits his employer's offices to meet the man-ager and fill out some final paperwork. There's a mounting sense of foreboding. The offices are located on a "narrow and deserted street in deep shadow" and "dead silence." Marlow enters through "immense double doors standing ponderously ajar," climbs a staircase, and comes to a waiting room where two women dressed in black guard the door to the manager's office. The atmosphere gets even darker. "I began to feel slightly un-easy," confesses Marlow. "I am not used to such ceremonies, and there was something ominous in the atmosphere. It was just as though I had been let into some conspiracy—I don't know—something not quite right; and I was glad to get out."

But the interview isn't over. The company requires Marlow to have a consultation with a doctor, who takes his pulse, then asks him, "with a certain eagerness," if he'd mind having his head measured. Marlow, rather surprised, agrees. The doctor then produces a pair of calipers and proceeds to appraise various dimensions of his skull, taking careful notes all the while.

"I always ask leave, in the interests of science, to measure the crania of those going out there," says the doctor.

"And when they come back too?" Marlow asks him.

"Oh, I never see them," the doctor replies, "and, moreover, the changes take place inside, you know."

I liked the agitated, portentous tone of this scene. I liked the idea of someone having their head measured before going on a dangerous journey, and I liked the idea that they never come back. The rest of the book made no sense to me.

But during my tutorial, everything changed. My tutor, Lyndall Gordon, sitting in a deep armchair, brought the story to life. The *Heart of Darkness* she described that rainy afternoon sounded nothing like the dry tome I'd been struggling with. Her *Heart of Darkness* was a gruesome, disturbing story about cannibals, slaves, nightmares, morbid rituals, and severed heads on stakes.

"It's just your cup of tea," she said, in her lovely South African accent, knowing how much I loved horror stories. This *Heart of Darkness* was immeasurably more mysterious and compelling than the book I'd been trying to read. How could I have missed those severed heads on stakes?

When I'd first confessed to Lyndall—who shaped and framed my love of literature—that I wanted to be an academic like her, she shook her head.

"Oh, no, I don't see you in that role at all," she said.

I was surprised and dismayed, but I can see why she responded as she did. I even saw it at the time. I had an enormous capacity for self-discipline, but I didn't identify with authority or with established ways of doing things. I could be oppositional, sometimes to an extreme degree. I was odd and unpredictable, and although I could certainly be described as eccentric, I wasn't eccentric in the academic way, in the sense that I wasn't detail oriented. I didn't care enough about getting the footnotes right.

Looking back, I wasn't ready for *Heart of Darkness*. Lyndall

Donald

Vincent

Turk

J.D.

Kevin

Sig

Charles

Guy Steven

Mikita

The Maximum Security Book Club: Original Configuration

understood this. The novella seemed complicated, she told me, if you weren't used to reading prose like Conrad's. You had to immerse yourself in it to really understand how it worked.

I went back to my room fired up with the desire to try again. I did. It was still impossible. But now it was interesting.

Over the past twenty-five years, I've read this book many times, and now I understand that, just as certain pieces of music can't be understood until you've heard them over and over again, some books need to be read more than once, and *Heart of Darkness* is one of them. Every time I read it, I seem to find a new and amazing passage I hadn't really paid attention to before. This slim novella seems magically self-renewing, like the loaves and the fishes. I know it's a book I'd want in my cell if I were in prison, which is one of the reasons why I chose it for the book club. Another reason I chose it is because I felt that if the men managed to struggle through Conrad's notoriously complex sentences, they might enjoy the gruesome, disturbing parts of the story. Perhaps they might even find some connections between Marlow's expedition into Africa and their own experiences at JCI and other prisons. But I never lost sight of the fact that it had taken me a long time to love it. This wasn't a book that opened itself up on first reading, and I hoped the prisoners would be patient. After all, I thought, the one thing they had plenty of was time.

JANUARY 9, 2013

By the time the book club had its first meeting, I was starting to feel a little more confident walking through the prison compound. Officers would recognize me from the classes I'd taught before and give me a nod; the sally port would open automatically as I approached with my escort, and if I heard someone yell a greeting on the compound, I'd give them a vague, friendly wave rather than staring blankly ahcad, as I used to do. I was no longer a nervous, naïve outsider, and I was cautiously optimistic for my next venture. Vincent had selected nine men for the book club whom he knew to be trustworthy and intelligent, and I'd asked him, when he enrolled them, to lay down the ground rules: no disrespect, no interrupting, no inappropriate behavior, and no reading ahead.

Heart of Darkness begins with five men on the deck of a yacht anchored in the Thames, waiting for the tide to turn. Marlow, sitting cross-legged by the mast, starts to tell a story. This opening scene came to my mind when I got to our classroom for the first session of the group and saw the men had set up a circle of chairs in preparation for our meeting. A central chair, saved for me, formed the anchor. Over the months and years I spent with this group of men, I noticed that—until we came to the final book—they always sat faithfully in the place they chose that very first day. Clearly, these were men who were accustomed to sticking to a routine and to carving out the boundaries of their own space, however small.

I noticed most of the men were wearing brown Timberland work boots, and a couple of them had small cartons of milk or orange juice on the floor by their chairs. A friendly Labrador retriever lay at the feet of the young man on my left, Steven, who was taking part in a program called Canine Partners for Life, which places dogs with responsible prisoners who train them for a year to work as service animals. Steven's dog was already so well trained he wouldn't even touch a treat placed on his paw until given the go-ahead. Confusingly, the dog was also named Steven. (The dogs' names are chosen by their sponsors, and this particular sponsor was financing a pair of dogs named in honor of his two sons.)

I began the discussion by telling the men a little about the life of Joseph Conrad and his ordeal in the Congo. I'd brought along a copy of his *Congo Diary*, and I read them the description of his journey upriver: dead bodies in his path, a skeleton tied to a tree, the grave of a nameless white man (a pile of stones in the sign of a cross). Then his body started to fail him. I read a passage from a letter he wrote to his aunt: "My health is far from good. In going up the river I suffered from fever four times in two months, and then at the Falls . . . I suffered an attack of dysentery lasting four days." Back in London after hovering at the brink of death, he was hospitalized with gout, neuralgia, malaria, and all the symptoms of physical and mental breakdown. "Utterly demoralized," he wrote in his journal. "I had the time to wish myself dead over and over again with perfect sincerity." He never fully recovered from the expedition, and was plagued for the rest of his life by recurrent fever and attacks of depression.

I handed each of the men a copy of *Heart of Darkness*, a bare-bones edition of the novella that I'd bought online (ten copies for twelve dollars, including shipping). I also handed them each a copy of a rather primitive map I'd made of Marlow's journey upriver and back. I suggested we go around the circle, each of the men reading aloud from the novel in turn, as much as they felt like reading. (I offered the chance to take a pass, but no one did.)

Kevin, a middle-aged man with thick glasses and a bushy gray beard, volunteered to go first. He began reading aloud with a grim, conscious effort, straining to pronounce the words, which came slowly and with difficulty. Everyone seemed relieved when he stopped after a few lines. Next was Vincent.

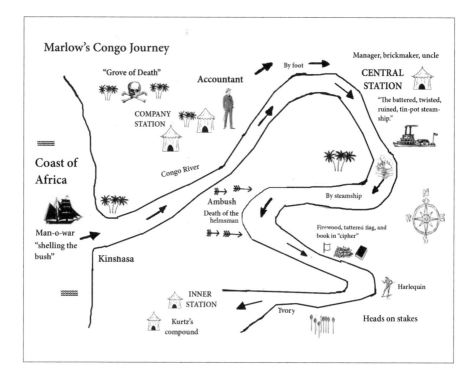

Marlow's Congo Journey

"Grove of Death"

Manager, brickmaker, uncle

Accountant

By foot

CENTRAL
STATION

"The battered, twisted,
ruined, tin-pot steam-
ship."

COMPANY
STATION

Coast of
Africa

Congo River

Man-o-war
"shelling the
bush"

Kinshasa

Ambush
Death of the
helmsman

By steamship

Firewood, tattered flag, and
book in "cipher"

Harlequin

INNER
STATION

Kurtz's
compound

Ivory

Heads on stakes

Putting on a pair of large, thick-lensed reading glasses, he picked up where Kevin had left off, and read articulately, at an even pace. Next came Steven. Six feet tall and two hundred pounds, his shoulders pumped up with prison muscle, Steven was all youth and energy. He read in a loud voice and squirmed around in his seat while he did so, bouncing his feet up and down on the floor. His section included a famously impressionistic passage in which Marlow's method of storytelling is described as "one of these misty halos that sometimes are made visible by the spectral illumination of moonshine." When he came to these lines, Steven's whole body twitched visibly. He looked up at me.

"I love that!" he said.

Later in *Heart of Darkness*, Marlow, deep in the uncharted Congo, comes across a twenty-five-year-old Russian, the son of an archpriest, dressed in a harlequin's colorful patchwork. Marlow is astonished to find him there. "His very existence was improbable, inexplicable . . ." This wasn't far from how I felt about Steven. To meet someone who's always upbeat is rare enough in the outside world; in a maximum security prison, it felt marvelously unlikely. I'd have expected anyone in Steven's circumstances to be cold, guarded, and cynical; but, like the Russian harlequin, "there he was gallantly, thoughtlessly alive, to all appearance indestructible . . ."

STEVEN

Steven was a real chatterbox: he found it difficult to keep quiet for much longer than ten minutes at a stretch. When he wasn't speaking, he was writhing and fidgeting. (He told me that he'd been diagnosed with ADD/ADHD when he was five, but thought it was "bullshit.") When I got to know him better, I learned there wasn't much point starting the discussion until he got there. His energy charged the atmosphere. He'd walk into the room with his big grin, his blue eyes gleaming. He liked to change up his hairstyle. Some days his light brown hair was combed flat, sometimes it was tucked under a cap or bandana, or, like today, it would be spiked into a short Mohawk. He always had a cheerful comment to brighten the room. "Hello! It's Wednesday, my favorite day of the week," he'd say. "The sun's shining," or "It's spaghetti for dinner," or "They're showing the Winter Olympics on TV next week." He'd often thank me after class too: "Hey, I just want to say I really felt like I learned a lot today." Every man played a role in the book club, but Steven was its beating heart.

And his enthusiasm wasn't directed only at the reading group. Steven threw himself into everything he did: college classes, playing his guitar, meditation, soccer, video games, Dungeons & Dragons, poker—even, believe it or not, the prison food. Although he kept up conscientiously with the books I assigned, he also read fiction by Lovecraft, Tolkien, and George R. R. Martin, and confessed to having a soft spot for Anne Rice's erotic fantasies. He corresponded with a mentor who taught him about occult subjects—"philosophy, psychology, how to control your own actions and the inner workings of your mind." Steven was a student of Magick, which he described to me as "understanding the different natures of energy types and thought patterns to be aware and prepared to act effectively in given situations."

Yet it wasn't only his youth and natural temperament that kept his spirits high. It was also the fact that, unlike most of the other men in the group, Steven would be getting out. When I first met him, he was three years into a thirteen-year sentence for armed robbery—a sentence that was harsher than usual due to the fact that he'd been in prison before, for first-degree burglary ("I did four and a half on six"). When I asked him about his current conviction, he told me he and four younger friends had gone to the home of a guy who'd taken $325 from Steven's sister with the promise of bringing her drugs. Steven had kicked open the apartment door, pointed a BB gun at the guy, and ordered him and another guy to get on the ground. When they left, they took an Xbox and a couple of cell phones. The cops picked them up right away, and Steven's friends, who were in their teens and had no criminal records, fingered him as the instigator. Steven never went to trial. He took a plea bargain for thirteen years. It seemed like a ridiculous sentence for what was basically a petty and juvenile crime—although, of course, I had only Steven's side of the story. If somebody had kicked down my apartment door and threatened me with a gun, I might very well see things differently.

For the rest of our allotted time—an hour and a half—the men asked me questions about Conrad and the colonization of the Congo. In preparation for our next meeting, I asked them to read the next section of *Heart of Darkness* on their own and to write a page about their thoughts. I liked the fact that we'd be reading the book in sections over a few weeks. In the days between our meetings, I hoped the men might also take the time to reflect on what we'd covered so far, perhaps returning to earlier parts of the book that hadn't been so clear.

JANUARY 16, 2013

I was upbeat when I got to the prison, and glad to find myself a chair that wasn't cracked. The book club seemed to be off to a great start. The men, I thought, had seemed genuinely interested in the opening of *Heart of Darkness*. This may have been true. But if it was, their interest had quickly waned. The book, they told me now, was monotonous and depressing. Conrad's long words and endless sentences made it impossible for them to understand what was going on. They had to have a dictionary beside them while they read.

"For one thing, you can tell this guy's not a native speaker," observed Sig, a prisoner whose gentle manner contrasted with his intimidating size. Whenever I saw his six-foot-six body squashed into the schoolroom furniture, I was reminded of a magician placing his assistant into a box that folds over into a smaller and smaller square. I was starting to see how all the chairs had come to be broken.

The oldest member of the group, Charles, agreed with Sig.

"I've been taking a writing class with Mr. Hall, and he tells us that a good writer comes straight to the point," said Charles. His tired blue eyes were set deep in a coarse, grizzled face, while tattoos of thorns and roses decorated his thin, pale arms. "This guy still hasn't got to the point after twenty-seven pages. There were forty-four words that I had to look up in the dictionary."

I tried to explain to the men what I'd found so difficult to understand myself: that Conrad was trying to give life to what he called "the commonplace surface of words," and the alienated, foreign quality of his prose made Marlow's character even more opaque. But to men not used to reading even naturalistic prose, it was hard to argue that a writer might not want to be clear. Charles saw Conrad's wordiness as a smoke screen, a way of drawing things out unnecessarily. The other prisoners agreed.

"The long words didn't bother me at first," said Steven. "I was starting to get excited about Marlow going to this unexplored place, but then after a while, the language started to get in the way. I got stuck when he got to that long part about rivets."

"Me too. I'm hoping he manages to find those rivets and finally get moving," muttered Charles.

In the jungle, Marlow runs into a man he refers to as the Accountant, a European dressed in British finery, with a "high, starched collar" and "white cuffs." He claims to admire the man. "I respected his collars, his vast cuffs, his brushed hair . . . That's backbone," Marlow declares. Since he's usually so cynical about the European colonizers, I asked the men if they thought Marlow was being sarcastic about the Accountant.

"For sure," said Steven. "I mean, he's got the time to starch his shirts. That's not backbone. That means he's got way too much time on his hands. There's all this shit going on around him, and what's he doing? He's looking after his shirts. To me, that's a kind of arrogance. That's vanity, not backbone."

"Don't you like to be neat and tidy?" I asked him.

"Sure," he said. "I mean, to a degree. But in here, after a while, you realize there's no point. You stop shaving. Some guys even stop taking showers. I used to save up to buy outside clothes. Now I don't even think about it; I just wear what they give me."

At JCI, you received the standard-issue prison uniform: one pair of shoes, one coat, one hat, one pair of jeans, two blue shirts (one long- and one short-sleeved), two pairs of white boxer shorts, two white T-shirts, one pair of long johns, and two pairs of socks. Most items were replaced every six months, except the shoes. You got new shoes once a year. Beyond that, you were allowed to order clothes in certain colors and styles from authorized companies, but you had to wear a blue shirt with "DPSCS" stamped on the back to distinguish you from the COs at a distance, in case of a fight or a riot. Many of the prisoners had a very limited wardrobe, and I became familiar with some of their staples: Vincent's "Italy" T-shirt, Charles's hand-patched sweatpants, J.D.'s gleaming white Adidas training shoes.

"When I first got to prison, I used to wear my suit every Sunday for church, with a lavender tie," confessed Vincent. "Back in the day, I dressed like a hippie: bright colors, all that. I used to get up on Sundays, shave, put on my suit. I gave all that up years ago." He waved a hand in dismissal. "Now look at me. I don't even bother shaving. There's no point. I mean, who am I going to run into? Nobody I haven't seen before, right?"

Guy, one of the younger men, was the only person who didn't think Marlow was being sarcastic about the Accountant.

"Bleaching and ironing your pants in the middle of the jungle," he said. "That's awesome!"

JANUARY 23, 2013

Outside the prison, if I mentioned I was reading *Heart of Darkness* with the prisoners, I usually got a strong reaction. A friend told me it was impossible to discuss the book properly without tackling the question of race. One of the other teachers in the prison program was a specialist on the Congo wars. He thought *Heart of Darkness* was a racist fantasy. When a local newspaper published an article on our work in the prison and entitled it "Heart of Darkness," he complained about it in our prison college program blog.

"Ever since Conrad used the phrase 'heart of darkness' to refer to the Congo," he wrote, "it's been the lazy go-to label for any place where affluent, mostly white folks go to try to help the natives and have their faith in humanity tested, including prisons."

I wondered if he was referring to me.

Although the men were struggling with Conrad's prose, I was enjoying the group's dynamic, and could feel myself growing more and more interested in the men; so I felt badly that they weren't getting much out of *Heart of Darkness*, and that reading the book was becoming such an uphill struggle.

When I got to our classroom the following week, Steven and his dog were the only ones there. It wasn't unusual for the men to arrive at different times. They came from various locations in the prison, and the COs could be neglectful about calling them. While we were setting up the chairs in a circle, I asked Steven about his family. He told me he was born and raised in Indian Head, Maryland, a small town on the Potomac River. His parents divorced when he was ten, and he lived with his father, who'd had various blue-collar jobs over the years. His younger sister, he said, had recently been released from a nearby women's prison for drug possession with intent to distribute. He'd also had three stepbrothers at different times, but his sister was the only sibling he was still in touch with. They talked a few times a month. He was also close to his dad, who came to visit him in jail and supported him financially. "I try to call him every week," he said. "He's the person I feel I've hurt the most."

Steven hadn't been in touch with his mother for years, apart from an "awkward and uncomfortable" phone call a few months earlier. "She's addicted to crack and she's currently in county jail," he said, sitting down and rubbing Steven the dog behind the ears. "I always thought to myself: I can't just leave her, because I have to take care of her and protect her, but now I've learned I can't sacrifice myself to save an unwilling party. It feels wrong and doesn't make sense and only causes even more grief."

"It doesn't sound like she's been much of a parent," I said.

"Maybe not," agreed Steven, "but whatever I've done, I've brought on myself. My problem is I like excitement. Fast cars, girls, danger, and no rules." Again, I thought of the Russian harlequin in *Heart of Darkness*, whose spirit is ruled, according to Marlow, by "the absolutely pure, uncalculating, unpractical spirit of adventure."

"What do you miss most from the outside?"

He laughed. "Do you really have to ask?"

Steven was girl crazy. The way he'd choose books from the prison library was by flicking through them to see if there were any sex scenes or descriptions of girls. I asked him if he had a girlfriend.

"She left me three months after I came to prison," he said. "She was pregnant."

"Did she have the baby?"

"That's a good question. See, her brother told me she had an abortion and moved back with her ex to Virginia, but a buddy of mine told me he saw a picture of her on Facebook, and she had a baby with her. So I don't know what's going on."

"Why did you break up?"

"We didn't break up. She moved away and never got back in touch with me. I tried to find out where she went but I couldn't get her new number. Eventually I just stopped trying. I gave up. I figured there was no point."

After this episode, Steven realized he needed to change. He decided he'd been living a pretty selfish life. Now, he told me, he felt compelled to go in the other direction, to abide by a personal code of honor "similar to the romantic, chivalrous knights of old." These days he believed in truth, courage, and discipline. As a dog trainer, he was held to higher standards than the other prisoners. "Responsibility used to be a big problem for me," he said. "So I work on that the most, and expect those around me to do the same. Sometimes I get prejudiced about those kinds of judgments."

When he'd been a student in my psychology class, Steven had confessed that his Achilles' heel was a tendency to self-sabotage—to violate his own internal parole. He was always getting into trouble. He seemed driven to forge and break rules with equal intensity. No one ever tormented him, it seemed, as much as he tormented himself. Yet I also remember him boasting about his ability to manipulate psychiatrists, and for the first time I started to wonder whether his enthusiasm might not be calculated. Was he feigning interest in *Heart of Darkness*, telling me what I wanted to hear, stringing me along? I'm not a pushover, but I do tend to trust people—even convicted felons—until they give me a reason not to. Perhaps Steven was taking advantage of me. But to what end? There wasn't anything I could do for him. I didn't give grades, and I wasn't girlfriend material. The only things he ever asked me for were a letter for his parole file and a pad of writing paper, neither of which seemed inappropriate. Other men had asked for more.

Meanwhile, our progress with *Heart of Darkness* seemed to be as slow and obstacle-ridden as Marlow's journey up the Congo. While no one gave up on it entirely—at least, not to my knowledge—some of the men admitted they were skipping "the boring parts," and when I asked Steven's cellmate, Guy, for his response to the week's reading, he had little to say.

"I wasn't really feeling this chapter," he mumbled, putting his head down on his tray table. I'd already noticed Guy could be moody, so I let it go, asking the same question of Sig, who often seemed to have interesting things to say.

"There were only certain passages that got through to me," he said.

"Can you remember any of them?"

"Okay. Yeah. Hold on. Let me find it. It's that part where they're on the boat, and that guy's just been shot by an arrow."

"You must mean the helmsman," I said.

"Right, the helmsman. And Marlow's wondering about the cannibals—how they can go so long without food. It's the part about hunger. Here it is. I've found it."

"Could you read it for us?"

Sig cleared his throat, and found the line on the page with his finger. "'Don't you know,'" he read, awkwardly, "'the devilry of lingering starvation, its exasperating torment, its black thoughts, its sombre and brooding ferocity? Well, I do . . . It's really easier to face bereavement, dishonour, and the perdition of one's soul—than this kind of prolonged hunger.'" He closed the book and looked up. "I thought that was really accurate. That's what hunger does to you. Anybody in prison will tell you that."

"But they feed you in here, don't they?"

"They give us food, if you can call it that. But it's the same thing, day in, day out. That's what makes you go crazy."

"Really?" I was surprised. After all, they were fed three meals a day and could buy themselves snacks and treats from the commissary.

"You don't feel that way at first," explained Vincent, who'd been in prison for more than thirty years and had a lifer's perspective. "At first, say the first five to seven years, you're still focused on your former life. And if you're young, that's usually girls, sex, and partying. That's what you dream about. After the first seven years or so, you lose that connection to the outside, and that's when you start yearning for friends and family, especially if they've stopped visiting you or if they're getting old. Then, after about fifteen years, food becomes the number one priority. You think about it constantly. You dream about it. Guys like me who've been in here for a while, we love to watch cooking shows on television. They help us remember things we've forgotten, how things used to taste."

"Yeah," agreed Sig. "But then the show ends and then you've gotta go stand in line for chopped-up mystery meat and watered-down gravy. And you should see some of the guys working in the kitchens here. They never shampoo their hair. They never take a shower. They don't even wash their hands after using the bathroom."

"Come on. It's not so bad. The spaghetti's great," objected Steven, who was clearly still at the first of Vincent's three stages.

"What did you make of the chapter, Steven?" I asked, trying to get us back to *Heart of Darkness*.

Steven looked down at his page of scribbled notes. "Well, see, I'm starting to think of this book as like a video game," he said. "You could call it 'Persistence' or something like that. You want to be the last one left. The helmsman was like one of the tools Marlow had, like an ax or a knife or something. Now he's going to have to go on without it."

Charles was struck by the moment after the helmsman is killed when Marlow realizes his shoes are filled with blood.

"I saw a guy die in front of me like that once," he said. "It was in San Quentin, the summer of 1970. We were all on lockdown. I was in my cell, talking to my buddy through the bars. He was outside on the tier because he was a kitchen worker, and kitchen workers didn't have to be locked down. Suddenly, these black guys dropped down over the side of the fourth tier and started stabbing my friend. He just fell to the ground right in front of my cell. There was nothing I could do. I just stood there and watched him bleed out on the ground."

Charles had a flat, matter-of-fact way of talking—he wasn't the type to show much emotion—but something in his voice suggested the incident had made a deep impression on him. In the brief silence that followed, I tried to imagine what it would feel like to watch a friend bleed to death in front of me and not be able to do a single thing to help.

Suddenly, Guy lifted up his head from the tray table.

"Those guys are cannibals, right?" he asked. "So how come they don't eat the helmsman?"

"Marlow doesn't give them a chance. It's the first paragraph on top of the page there," I replied, thankful to be getting back to territory I was more comfortable with. " 'I had made up my mind that if my late helmsman was to be eaten, the fishes alone should have him.' "

"Yeah, but Marlow's on his own, and there's a big gang of cannibals, right? I mean, they could have got there first."

"So why do you think they didn't eat him, Guy?"

"Maybe it went against the rules," he said.

"The rules?" I repeated. "What rules?"

"Cannibal rules," said Guy.

"Cannibal rules?"

"Yeah. Like, maybe you can only eat somebody you've killed."

"I'm afraid I don't know much about cannibal etiquette," I said.

"We had a cannibal here once," Kevin recalled. "Any of you guys remember Tiny? When they arrested him, they found these body parts in his fridge. He'd been eating these hookers he'd killed."

"Big fat guy, right?" recalled Sig. "Yeah. What happened to him?"

"They sent him to the supermax up in Cumberland."

"He wasn't fat when he came in," Sig said, turning to me to explain, "but he got real big in prison. It's the food they serve here. A lot of guys get fat in jail. Thing is, if you're eating this much fat and starch, you've got to work out."

Trying to steer the conversation back once again to *Heart of Darkness*, I asked the men for their thoughts about Kurtz, the German colonizer rumored to have "gone native" in the depths of the jungle.

"Marlow's heard all these people claiming that Kurtz must have gone mad," I said, "but Marlow says there's nothing wrong with his mind. 'I wasn't arguing with a madman . . . ,' he says. 'Believe me or not, his intelligence was perfectly clear— concentrated, it is true, upon himself with horrible intensity, yet clear . . . But his soul was mad. Being alone in the wilderness, it had looked within itself, and, by heavens! I tell you, it had gone mad.'"

"That's what happens to guys in the lockup," said Sig. "I seen it with my own eyes."

"It's like that dude that got killed over at the Cut," said Kevin. "What did they call him?"

"Homeland Security," somebody said.

"Right, Homeland Security," recalled Kevin. "This guy was, like, the ultimate CO. Just the worst, man. They stabbed him to death. Then everybody painted him out like he was this great big hero and all this shit. They said there were over two thousand people at his funeral."

"So how was this guy like Mr. Kurtz?" I asked. I was having trouble keeping the discussion focused. The men would constantly get sidetracked, and their stories were so bizarre and outrageous I always wanted to hear more.

"I guess he was just doing his job," said Steven. "I mean, when you look at prison from the outside perspective, especially a place like the Cut, there's all this violence and horror. But from this guy's perspective, maybe it was just work. Maybe Mr. Kurtz thought he was just doing his job."

"Right. It's his job—but he gets over-involved in it. To Kurtz, it's personal," I said. "I think that's the difference between Marlow and Kurtz. Marlow doesn't go all the way. Look at what Marlow says about Kurtz. 'He had made that last stride, he had stepped over the edge . . . ,' while Marlow's been permitted to draw back his 'hesitating foot.' Kurtz hurls himself into 'the bottom of a precipice where the sun never shines,' while Marlow merely 'peeped over the edge.'"

JANUARY 30, 2013

Modern editions of *Heart of Darkness* often include the famous essay by the African author Chinua Achebe, "An Image of Africa: Racism in Conrad's 'Heart of Darkness.'" Perhaps the prisoners would have felt differently about *Heart of Darkness* if I'd introduced it as a notoriously racist book, but to me the story isn't about race but about a man who comes to face the truth about human nature and what this experience does to him. In fact, when Marlow first mentions "one of the dark places of the earth," he's referring not to Africa but to London. Marlow's journey is literal, but it's also symbolic and psychological. What distinguishes him from those that fall under the spell of darkness—

including Kurtz, and most of the European colonizers—isn't the color of his skin but his capacity for work.

After dragging his half-submerged steamer out of the Congo mud, Marlow has to repair the damage and make the boat fit to make the journey upriver, during which he has to keep the boiler stoked and the pipes from leaking. While he doesn't necessarily enjoy all this toil, he knows it's critical. The work absorbs his attention, keeping his mind from dwelling on the violence and cruelty of the colonizers. In other words, he's dedicated to his work not for itself but for what it precludes. "What saves us is efficiency—the devotion to efficiency," he claims.

This question of work was the subject of our final discussion of *Heart of Darkness*. Around half the prisoners at JCI had a job. Some worked in Dietary (preparing food in the kitchen), some in Maintenance (janitorial or cleaning jobs), and others worked on the grounds. Older guys who'd been at the prison for a long time—most of them maximum security prisoners— usually had the most enviable jobs, which were those in the license plate, wood, or sewing shops. Prisoners who worked in these factories started at a base salary of ninety cents an hour, and with training and experience they could earn up to a couple hundred dollars a month. There was also the Laundry, which paid wages comparable to the other workshops and had contracts to clean bedding for other prisons, hospitals, and institutions around the state from about a sixty-mile radius.

Sometimes the men managed to save a little money, although most of their earnings were spent in the commissary; the prison gave them nothing at all except a "wellness pack" (I misheard it as "welcome pack") when they first arrived that contained two sheets, a blanket, a towel, a washcloth, and a roll of toilet paper. After that, they had to buy everything for themselves, though prisoners who worked in the kitchen would often steal food to sell more cheaply on the tiers the same way some men sold stolen commissary goods out of their cells. And then, of course, there was the contraband brought in by officers, visitors, and staff—mainly cell phones and narcotics, which were sold to prisoners at a substantial profit.

Most of the men agreed with Marlow's opinions about work—that it could bring you a sense of purpose, a kind of order and stability that could keep you grounded and out of trouble. For Marlow, life is tragic only at the rare moments when he becomes conscious of its lack of meaning. He occupies himself in his work with dignity and authenticity; he's engaged not by any particular outcome or desired result but by conscious immersion in the struggle itself. It's his devotion to work that allows him to return from the brink. I told the men that I thought these observations of Marlow's were the clearest part of the book, as though they were the only things he felt sure of, just as the steamer was the only thing he could trust. He certainly didn't trust language.

"I noticed that part where he complains about all the different words the whites use to describe the natives," said Donald, a surly-looking African-American who, so far, had hardly said a word. "They've got all those names for them. 'Enemies,' 'criminals,' 'workers,' 'rebels.' I thought of the word the COs use for us: 'inmates.' We don't like that word."

"Oh? What would you prefer to be called?"

"Incarcerated citizens," suggested Vincent.

"You can call me a convict, or a felon, or even a criminal," said Donald. "Don't matter to me."

"Does everyone prefer those words?" I asked.

"I think the overwhelming majority of men over thirty would prefer them," said Charles. "I don't know about the men under thirty. I don't think most of them would even know the difference."

" 'Inmate' is the term you hear most often," said Sig.

"But it's not *our* word," Donald pointed out. "It's *their* word. They try to be all friendly and polite, calling us 'sir' and 'gentlemen.' Don't call me a gentleman if you're not going to let me take a shit in private."

"So you don't trust language?" I asked him.

"Nope. That's why I don't say a lot," admitted Donald.

"Why not?"

"You're living through it every day. You don't want to talk about all the shit that goes down in here. What's the point?"

By now, although I'd spent a lot of time in the prison, I still had little sense of what the men's lives were like and how they'd been affected by their years of incarceration. I'd heard about acts of hostility and violence, but I didn't know how often they happened or how public they were. All I'd witnessed so far were the grinding indignities of everyday life in an underfunded and repressive institution.

The question of language was vital in *Heart of Darkness*, and we'd only just touched on it; but when I looked at my watch, I saw our hour and a half was almost up. Time always seemed to pass so quickly in that room. At least, it did for me. I felt as though we hadn't devoted enough attention to *Heart of Darkness*, and I also felt a little frustrated with the men for not being willing to grant Conrad the attention I felt he deserved.

"Before we finish, I want to look at one last passage, and it deals with precisely this subject: whether you can communicate your experience to other people," I said. "It's the passage where Marlow gets frustrated with his listeners. He's talking about Kurtz. He says, 'He was just a word for me. I did not see the man in the name any more than you do. Do you see him? Do you see the story? Do you see anything? It seems to me I am trying to tell you a dream . . .' He's talking about how language gives the illusion of bringing us closer, but it actually cuts us off from one another. Marlow actually says it explicitly at the end of this passage: 'We live, as we dream—alone . . .'"

I see *Heart of Darkness* as a study in existential despair, and in this sense it might not sound like the most appropriate book to bring to men facing life in prison. But if Marlow learns about despair, he also learns how to distract himself from it, and this is what I wanted the men to understand—and at moments I believe they did. Still, for the most part, they saw it as just a badly written book. I felt as though I really hadn't managed to convey to them how Conrad deliberately tries to make ordinary things seem strange, twisting words out of shape until you start to see them in a new way and think differently about what they do and how they work. It's the outsider—the foreigner like Conrad, the loner like Marlow—who can make us see our native language from a new perspective. Ironically, however, what Conrad shows us is our inability to make each other understand our experiences. I certainly hadn't been able to get across my own experience of *Heart of Darkness*, and now it was too late. The men were getting restless, and the CO was due to take the count. I felt frustrated with myself. It was as though I'd only just managed to skim the surface.

I asked the men for their final verdict on the book. They had very little to say. Even Steven faltered.

"I'm not a fan," he finally confessed.

The only prisoner with a substantial comment was Charles. "'To me," he said, "it felt like trying to put a puzzle together with a whole bunch of pieces that don't fit. You've finished the puzzle, and the picture don't make no sense. And what's more, you've got all these pieces left over."

I recall thinking much the same thing myself when I first encountered *Heart of Darkness*: that you could take out nine of every ten sentences, and the story, such as it was, would still get told. I found the style repetitive and overbearing, the protagonist unsympathetic and inscrutable. Yet, whenever I came back to it, more of the "in-between matter" made sense, and previously invisible pictures would start to take shape—images that eventually became more intriguing to me than the surface plot. My early struggles to make sense of these images were full of misunderstandings, and partly because of this it took me time to get comfortable with them. It took me many rereadings to appreciate the book's complexities and come to terms with Conrad's difficult prose. Even now I'm not sure how much I fully "understand" the book, and to what extent my "understanding"—any "understanding," perhaps—is essentially a confused projection.

"It was sort of like an abstract painting," continued Charles. "Everybody saw something different. That thing you said about language, for example. While you were talking, I was thinking, 'Why did she see that and I didn't?'"

"What did *you* see?" I asked him.

"Tell the truth, not much."

Though not surprised, I was disappointed.

"I'd give it three out of ten," Charles concluded. "And that's generous."

2

"BARTLEBY, THE SCRIVENER:

A STORY OF WALL STREET"

Until the age of fourteen, I was a tomboy with a reputation for trouble. I'd climb trees, sass teachers, fight boys, and once impressed my classmates by performing the legendary feat of jumping off the library roof. Yet, when I hit puberty, almost overnight I became awkward, self-conscious, and virtually inarticulate. I loved school, but my thriving was academic, not social. I read hungrily and wrote long, elaborate, carefully argued essays in a tiny script, but I couldn't talk about my ideas. My passive vocabulary was swollen and grotesque, but in the flesh I was another sullen teenager who spoke in monosyllables, or not at all. Impressed by my written work, teachers would question me directly in class. I'd sit mutely, frozen with shame, looking down at my book; if pressed, I'd blush violently and hide behind my hair. Nobody understood why I wouldn't respond. It was downright weird.

I rationalized my withdrawal by telling myself I was above the idiots around me. To engage with the teachers' questions, I felt, would be to lower myself to their level. I was offended by their clumsy pedantry, their dull, one-dimensional readings of the books I loved. It never crossed my mind that I might have anything to learn from them or that I could have changed the level and direction of the discussion. Instead of admiring my teachers, as I'd always done before, I suddenly found myself at odds with them. I became a brooding enemy. My real fear, which I no doubt grasped at some level, was that my replies to their questions would emerge as mumbled platitudes. Aloof silence was more in line with what I wanted to express. I identified not with my voice, but with my writing, and was as unwilling to be judged by my faltering, half-baked banalities as by my hair, teeth, or skin. I didn't speak, because whenever I opened my mouth, I sounded stupid. I couldn't think and speak at the same time. Sitting down to write, I was calm. Things were in their place. The world was as it should be.

Many years later, when I told my friend Ari about my mute years, he compared me to Bartleby. We were both teaching at Eastern Mediterranean University in Northern Cyprus, and after classes were over we'd sometimes take a walk together through the old town of Famagusta. On this occasion we were walking from the Church of St. George of the Greeks to the Tanners' Mosque. We'd just seen a pigeon that had no feathers from the neck up, and we'd both thought the bird looked—there was no other word for it—embarrassed.

"Who's Bartleby?" I asked.

"You've never heard of Bartleby? 'Bartleby, the Scrivener'?" Ari was taken aback.

"Is he in Dickens?" I ventured.

"No!" He sounded indignant. " 'Bartleby, the Scrivener': it's a story by Herman Melville. The author of *Moby-Dick*. I assume you've heard of *Moby-Dick*?"

"Of course," I said, "though I haven't read it. You shouldn't take it for granted that everybody's familiar with American literature."

"I don't," he said. "There are just certain books I assume everyone's read—everyone with any claims to a higher education, at least. 'Bartleby' is one of those books. It's a cultural touchstone, like *Huckleberry Finn*, or *Hamlet*. You should read it, and not just so you don't seem so ignorant: I think you'd enjoy it."

"Oh? Why?"

"I think you'd be interested in Bartleby. He's a complete enigma. One day he just suddenly stops communicating with other people. He won't work. He won't do anything. Nobody understands him."

"Sounds to me like one of those stories where nothing ever happens," I said, unwilling to concede, although I generally deferred to Ari in matters of literary taste. As I suspected, he was right: I did like "Bartleby" when I read it, but that wasn't for a while.

Funnily enough, I recall the circumstances of our conversation very clearly—the featherless pigeon, the sunlight on the mosque—but I have no memory of first reading "Bartleby." At sixty-four pages, it's more of a novella than a tale, too long to be read in a single sitting, though it has the structural tightness of a short story. In some ways it seems linear and unified; in others, it's complex and circuitous. Although it's been interpreted as a religious parable, a study of the legal profession, a reflection of Melville's economically precarious career, and an attack on his father-in-law, it's essentially a nuanced and concentrated study of a pair of particularly intriguing characters: Bartleby and the man who gradually becomes obsessed with him.

I understand the narrator's fascination. I, too, find myself mysteriously drawn to Bartleby, in part because I recognize in him some of my own recessive antisocial tendencies. But we must be careful not to judge poor Bartleby—"pallidly neat, pitiably respectable, incurably forlorn!"—by his surface behavior. "Bartleby was one of those beings," writes the narrator, "of whom nothing is ascertainable, except from the original sources, and in his case those are very small."

I always had a difficult time knowing what to wear for the book club. At the orientation session for prison volunteers we'd been told that women had to be especially careful not to dress in a way that could be considered provocative. "Some of these men, they're hard-core sex offenders," said Sergeant Kelly, the tough-looking, short-haired African-American woman who was in charge of laying down the law to outsiders like me. "They be sitting there, and they be looking like they studying the assignment, but all the time they be trying to look down your top or get a peek up your skirt. That's why we say nothing above the knee. No miniskirts, no shorts, no open toes, no see-through, no spandex, no sleeveless."

I couldn't imagine ever breaking the dress code. Tight-fitting clothes make me feel uncomfortable, and I wouldn't be caught dead in spandex. Still, I managed to get into trouble more than once for my choice of attire. I've never been a fan of the colorless skirts and pantsuits many women wear to work, and I liked wearing bright clothes to provide some relief from the general bleakness of the prison. But when I wore a red corduroy skirt, I got called out on it, even though it was ankle length. As we walked through the yard, the CO who was escorting me reprimanded me for my fashion choice.

"Just for future reference," he said, "it's not a good idea to wear anything red here, especially not a skirt. You know what red does to a bull, right? We've got a lot of rapists and sexual offenders in here, and I'm just saying, you might want to wear a different color. One day it might make a difference."

The COs, I'd noticed, liked to characterize the prisoners as hostile and dangerous: caged animals just waiting for the chance to attack. I thought they took pleasure in exaggerating the threat posed by the men, who, in my experience at least, were far more polite and deferential than the guards. Perhaps, by imagining this constant danger, the COs made their jobs seem more vital and exciting. Yet, in truth, they were the ones I found intimidating, with their batons, handcuffs, and cans of pepper spray hanging from their belts. And Sergeant Kelly was the scariest of them all.

"These men are all manipulators," she warned us. "Don't let them fool you, even if they look like the boy next door. They try to compromise you, and the first step in compromising you is to affect you mentally by trying to separate you from the officers. They want you to be on their side. They even act like they your friends."

I thought of the men in my book group. Some of them— Steven, Guy, or J.D., for example—could easily have been "the boy next door," especially since tattoos have become mainstream. But most of them looked, frankly, like criminals. On a bad hair day, Kevin looked like a cross between Charles Manson and the Unabomber. Donald, too, was the popular image of the criminal type: very big, very black, and very surly. At first I was intimidated by his appearance and Angry Man attitude, but it wasn't long before I began to intuitively sense he'd have my back if anything ever went down, a feeling I never had around the COs.

FEBRUARY 6, 2013

I'd ordered another discount, no-frills edition: "Bartleby" and "Benito Cereno," the texts and nothing more, small print on cheap paper, ten copies for sixteen dollars. "Bartleby" was published in 1853, so I realized some of the men might have difficulties with the archaic vocabulary, but I definitely didn't expect their problems to begin with the title. Although I pronounced it over and over again, the protagonist's name seemed to be a huge stumbling block. Kevin called him "Bart-lebby." Guy—possibly thrown off by my English accent—said "Bottleby." Most of the others wouldn't even attempt it, referring to Bartleby as "that guy" or "the guy with the weird name." I couldn't fathom what made Bartleby's name sound so strange to them, so off-putting, other than the fact that it was unfamiliar.

"It's easy to pronounce when you get used to it," I told them.

"Why would we want to get used to a weird-ass name like that?" wondered Turk, a middle-aged, light-skinned African-American.

I was a little offended.

"I have a cat called Bartleby," I reminded him.

"Hey, that's right! The Five Thousand Dollar Cat!" Turk recalled.

My cat had been a subject of controversy a couple of months ago, when I was teaching the psychology course. One day I'd ended class early because I had to go and pick up Bartleby from the pet emergency room, where he'd been in surgery after swallowing a dryer sheet. The operation to have the polyester fabric disentangled from his intestines had cost almost five thousand dollars, and the following week, when the men asked about my cat, I'd made the mistake of telling them the whole story. If they'd learned anything from that class, it was the story of my "Five Thousand Dollar Cat." (For my part, I'd learned the importance of pet insurance.)

When we read *Heart of Darkness*, we all began together; with "Bartleby," however, I'd asked the men to read the first section on their own. I asked them now how they'd enjoyed the beginning of the tale.

"This one kind of threw me for a loop," admitted Vincent.

"There were too many characters," confessed Guy. "I couldn't follow it."

"Too many characters?" I said, with surprise. "There's the narrator, and there's Bartleby. That's it, pretty much."

"What about that whole Ginger Nut thing?" said Guy.

"Okay. There are three other scriveners in the office along with Bartleby: Turkey, Nippers, and Ginger Nut," I said. "But it doesn't matter if you can't keep them straight. They're not really that important. Everyone else finished the first section, right?"

The men looked embarrassed. There was a general shuffling of feet. No one would meet my gaze. Finally, Steven spoke up.

"This was a big weekend, in case you didn't know."

"Oh?"

"Yeah. The Ravens won the Super Bowl," declared Vincent. "You're not from Baltimore—you're not even American—so there's no way you can understand how huge that is, Mikita. It's once in a lifetime. After the Super Bowl, I didn't care what happened to Bartleby."

A big difference I'd noticed between my college students and the prisoners was that my students, anxious about grades above all else, would try to bluff, claiming they'd done the reading when it was obvious that they hadn't. The prisoners, on the other hand, unversed in classroom decorum, would always be straight with me, and this was one of the things I liked about them. At first I was surprised when they didn't finish the reading, since they told me they enjoyed the book club so much. When I understood more about the men's living conditions, however, I realized I should have been surprised when they *had* done the reading. The prison was an echo chamber; everywhere, sound reverberated off metal surfaces and concrete walls. Public spaces were open and crowded, and there was usually a television playing nearby—if not in your cell, then in the one next door. Some of the men had earplugs, but I doubt they managed to cancel out the constant blare that rang through the tiers, even, apparently, at night.

"Let's talk about the part you read," I suggested, after the men had spent half our allotted time trying to educate me about the historic significance of the Ravens winning the Super Bowl. "What can you remember about it?"

"The main thing I thought was that it all felt kind of hopeless," said Guy. "The lawyer dude who hired this guy—he really had to struggle. He was obsessed. I mean, I just didn't get why he cared that much."

"So you didn't sympathize with the narrator?"

"No way!" he exclaimed.

"He's the wimpiest guy you've ever met!" said Kevin. The others were nodding in agreement. "I mean, isn't he supposed to be the boss? Why's he letting this idiot Bart-lebby walk all over him?"

From our previous conversations and a glance at his court docket, I knew Kevin had once been a boss himself. He'd headed a construction crew until his drug problem got out of hand, leading to a string of sad convictions: theft, burglary, destruction of property, possession of a deadly weapon, battery, violation of probation. He'd been a student in the first class I taught at the prison—a writing class—and I'd enjoyed his unguarded comments and cheerful demeanor. After that, however, he hadn't returned, and I'd assumed he wasn't especially interested in improving his writing. It turned out I'd been wrong. Kevin had loved the class, he told me, but he suffered from a seizure disorder, and for the last few months his seizures had been so bad, he hadn't been allowed off the tier.

Whenever that happened now, the other men in the group would take notes for Kevin, tell him what we talked about in class, and take him any handouts I made. This kind of behavior wasn't unusual. Within their own groups and gangs, the prisoners would do favors for one another: lend each other money, clothing, and books; help one another move to different cellblocks and obtain coveted work assignments; give advice on how to get various kinds of privileges; and shout encouraging messages to those in the segregation cells. Most important, they listened to one another's life stories and followed the endless ins and outs of one another's legal cases.

At fifty-one, Kevin was in poor health. He told me once that prison years are like dog years, except—instead of seven dog years for every human year—you have to add ten to a man's age to account for the toll on his health. What he said made sense, but I'd also read statistics showing that black men, at least, lived longer in prison than on the outside. Some lifers, I'd noticed, were unusually young looking for their age, since limited sun exposure delayed the normal signs of aging. Kevin was one of them. He had a boyish face behind his prison-issue glasses and

KEVIN

matted, wild-man beard. I sometimes wondered what he'd look like after a shave and a haircut, and once I asked him if he'd ever considered getting rid of his beard. In reply, he held up the prison ID that hung on a string around his neck. In the photo, he was clean-shaven, and his big jaw and scowling brow gave him a menacing, unhinged look. I then understood the point of the huge beard: to turn him from an angry felon into a friendly tramp.

Kevin was proud of his Irish origins, asserted by the "Erin Go Bragh" tattoo on his left arm, just below "Debra." He usually wore a beige baseball cap, the standard prison-issue blue short-sleeved work shirt with "DPSCS" on the back, heavy jeans, and brown Timberland work boots. He carried his books in a string laundry bag, and turned in homework that was scrawled on sheets ripped from a yellow legal pad, their edges frayed and torn. His handwriting, violent and chaotic, paid no attention to lines or margins, and he pressed down with such force that the back of each sheet felt as though it were covered in braille. And although everything was misspelled, what he wrote was always clear, heartfelt, and often unintentionally funny. At first I thought he wouldn't stick with the group. Not only did he miss half the meetings due to his seizures, he clearly wasn't a natural reader and found the books tough to follow. Yet, over time, he became one of the club's most ardent participants.

When I got home that evening and told David about the trouble the men had pronouncing Bartleby's name, he reminded me that when our cat had been sick, the staff at the animal hospital had experienced the same problem. Most of the time he was "Bartley" or "Barnaby," but I also remember getting a call from a vet tech with "an update on Bumblebee."

I named my young cat Bartleby because I liked the sound of the word, and because it made a nice match with my older cat, Queequeg, named after Ishmael's cannibal companion in *Moby-Dick*. But there's never been any of Melville's impenetrable scrivener in this playful and affectionate little creature. These days, eighteen-year-old Queequeg is the one who "prefers not to." Still, I suppose you could make the case that, to some degree, Melville's Bartleby has the stubbornness and perversity that some people believe to be characteristic of all cats. Fortunately, however—at least as far as we know—most cats don't seem to share the desolate scrivener's deep-rooted despair.

FEBRUARY 13, 2013

In the morning I got an e-mail from the librarian telling me the prison was on lockdown. This happened four or five times a year, usually for a week or so, sometimes just for random searches, sometimes due to an outbreak of a contagious illness, but most often as a result of a "10–10" (meaning a fight involving one or more COs). Occasionally just one wing or one tier was on lockdown and the prison stayed open; when this happened, men in the locked unit wouldn't be allowed to leave their cells. This particular lockdown was unusually long; in the end, it lasted thirteen days. Later, I learned there'd been a big fight the day after I was last at the prison. Four COs had been injured; one had yet to return to work. (He might have quit, been fired, or been assigned to another institution; no one seemed to know.) The lockdown, according to the men, was a form of retaliation on the part of the prison authorities.

I spent the day at home, caring for my own little Bartleby— still recovering from his surgery—and trying to understand why I found Melville's odd story so intriguing. I read an article written in 1965 by a psychiatrist who thought autism should be called "the Bartleby complex," a suggestion that obviously never caught on, probably because it didn't sound clinical enough. I was glad. It would have gone against the grain of "Bartleby." Anyway, Bartleby isn't typical of anything; he's a specific person in a particular situation. Anyone who thinks they can understand him from his surface behavior is making the same mistake as the narrator. Bartleby can't be so easily read.

The story's opacity fascinates and frustrates me to almost the same degree. What's especially perplexing about it is that it doesn't give us what we expect from first-person fiction, which is access to the workings of the narrator's consciousness. Instead of getting to know the narrator from the inside out, we learn almost nothing about him at all except for the few details he chooses to share, such as the fact that he is "one of those unambitious lawyers who never addresses a jury," he's known for his prudence, he once worked for "the late John Jacob Astor," he's currently a "Master in Chancery," and his second-floor office is furnished with a "bust of Cicero."

With real people, including intimate friends, even lovers, we always run into something that stops us from getting to know them completely: blind spots, veils, projections, misunderstandings. What makes first-person fiction so rewarding and pleasurable to read is the fact that our insight into the narrator's consciousness isn't hampered by such occlusions. In this sense, "Bartleby" is less like fiction than real life. At the end of the story, Bartleby and the narrator are even more mysterious than they were at the beginning. We never learn exactly who they are or how they came to be that way.

FEBRUARY 20, 2013

We next met on the day the men were finally allowed out of their cells after the thirteen-day lockdown. As a group, they seemed—unsurprisingly—chastened and defeated. I tried to imagine what it would feel like being locked in a six-by-eight-foot room for thirteen days with another person, getting my food handed to me through a slot in the door, eating in front of an open toilet, constant noise echoing down the tier, with no idea how long the lockdown was going to last. Trapped in their cells for so long, the men had all finished "Bartleby." Guy had even read it twice.

"That's great." I was genuinely pleased. "Good for you."

"It was the only thing I had to read," he complained. "I was so bored, I was reading candy wrappers."

"So does it make any more sense to you now?" I asked him.

"No," he said sourly.

"One thing me and Guy were talking about is how Bartleby doesn't really do anything, but he causes all this trouble," said Steven, who was Guy's cellmate. "It shows you how saying and doing nothing can be a way of showing your power. We were comparing it to this lockdown."

"There was no reason for it," added Donald. "It was just retaliation, just to show us who's in charge."

"They didn't have to keep us on lockdown for thirteen days," said Donald's pal Turk. "They did it because they can. They just refused to open the cell doors."

"They preferred not to," added Charles.

As the men went on venting their frustration about the lockdown, I wondered about this analogy. They'd made an interesting connection, I thought, and on the surface it seemed astute; but at the same time I couldn't help thinking they were using it as a reason to talk about the lockdown rather than about "Bartleby." Their logic was always loose and associative: they could only talk about "Bartleby" by making connections with their own experience, and it was starting to frustrate me. I tried to let go of my own thoughts and feelings about the book, focusing instead on what I was hearing from the men; but the more I listened, the more irritated I grew. Intelligent discussion about a book doesn't preclude personal anecdotes, but the men's stories seemed to have only a very oblique connection with the text. In other words, they weren't actually talking about "Bartleby" at all, but making "Bartleby" talk about them. Absurdly, this made me feel sad on Bartleby's behalf, as though—once again—he was being neglected. Melville's words hold Bartleby in a frame, enclosing and locating him, and I felt a need to consider these words as a way of attending to Bartleby's suffering. But the men didn't want to look at Melville's words. They wanted to use their own.

"Can we get back to Bartleby?" I interrupted them. "What do you think made him behave the way he did?"

"I thought about that a lot," said Steven, who seemed to be intent on finding clues to the mystery. "I guess he wanted attention. He wanted the narrator to get pissed at him instead of being such a wuss."

"But the narrator *does* get pissed at him," I argued.

"He does?"

"Yes," I said. "He's repelled by him, but he doesn't react the way you'd expect. Look at the paragraph in the middle of the page. He says, 'So true it is, and so terrible too, that up to a certain point the thought or sight of misery enlists our best affections; but, in certain special cases, beyond that point it does not.' He's saying that when we meet somebody who's suffering and we can't do anything about it, we start to suffer as well. But when things get to a certain point, we realize—maybe unconsciously—that our suffering is completely useless and counterproductive, so we make it stop by rejecting them. 'To a sensitive being, pity is not seldom pain. And when at last it is perceived that such pity cannot lead to effectual succor'—that means, when we can't provide effective help—'common sense bids the soul be rid of it.'"

I wanted to ask the men whether they understood what the narrator meant in this passage. I wanted to know whether they'd ever had an experience with such a "special case," or whether they might have actually been such a "case" themselves. But my exegesis of the passage had produced nothing but a loud sniff and a couple of yawns, and I knew there was no point pushing the men to focus on the parts of the story I found so compelling if they didn't find those parts interesting themselves. Too, the more enthusiastic I got about the story, the more I sensed the men were resisting my enthusiasm, refusing to engage either with me or with "Bartleby." Later, I recalled that the narrator refers to Bartleby's periods of silent refusal as "his profoundest dead-wall reveries" because the scrivener stands immobile before a window that looks directly out on "a lofty brick wall, black by age and everlasting shade." Bartleby himself, I realized, was on a kind of self-induced, permanent lockdown.

When I thought about "Bartleby" in these terms, I started to understand why men facing life in prison might not get especially excited when asked to read about somebody who stands staring at a wall all day. I also began to notice uncomfortable parallels between my own naïve desire to share "Bartleby" with the men and the narrator's inability to leave Bartleby alone even when he makes it clear he doesn't want to be helped. Was I coming to the prison not for the sake of the men but to fill myself with what the narrator refers to as "delicious self-approval"? Was I in fact concerned with feeling superior to others—braver, tougher, more compassionate and altruistic? Asking myself such questions made me feel distinctly uneasy. Perhaps they'd hit upon an ugly truth.

I left the prison feeling anxious; to make things worse, I had to drive straight into work for two meetings, one after another, and I'd forgotten my wallet. Unable to buy lunch or even coffee, I had to get through the day on the strength of a handful of dried cranberries I found in my car.

FEBRUARY 27, 2013

We had one more session on "Bartleby," and when I got to the classroom, I had a shock. Steven was miserable. Of course, it shouldn't have been so much of a surprise: no one can be constantly enthusiastic, especially not in circumstances such as his. Still, I was disturbed to see the always upbeat young man slumped unhappily in his chair. Then I noticed his dog was missing.

"What's wrong?" I asked him. "Where's Steven?"

"I lost my dog privileges," he said.

"Oh, no!" My mind immediately rushed to my own dog, Grisby. The thought of having him taken away from me was unbearable, and for an awful moment I thought I was going to burst into tears. I sat down next to Steven to hear the story.

"What happened?"

"I messed up."

"What did you do?" I assumed he must have been caught with contraband: drugs, alcohol, maybe even a gun.

"I went back for a second dinner," he confessed sheepishly.

"Are you kidding?"

"It's an infraction."

"Like Oliver Twist?"

"Yeah. Whatever." A couple of years later, when I asked the men if they had any ideas for the book club, Steven mentioned that he still hadn't read *Oliver Twist*. It was, I now realize, presumptuous of me to assume he'd understood my reference to the character, as it had been presumptuous of Ari to assume I was familiar with Bartleby.

"So what's going to happen to Steven?" I asked.

"They've given him to Guy. He's also a dog trainer."

"And Guy's your cellmate, right?"

"Not anymore. They've moved me to E Building."

I could tell Steven was suffering. He and his dog had been a special pair, partly due to their twinned names, but also because of the bond that had developed between them. Steven had told me that he'd been getting used to prison life until the dog-training program started. As soon as he'd bonded with Steven the dog, however, he'd realized what he was missing, and how desperate he was for affection.

"Now I know that I want to work with animals after I'm released," he told me. "Probably dogs or horses."

I brought him some information about colleges with vet tech training programs, but with a felony conviction behind him, Steven wasn't sure he'd qualify for a loan.

"Anyway," he said, rolling up the material I'd handed him, "you don't need college for what I want to do."

"What's that?"

"I want to be one of those guys that goes round to peoples' house and traps critters that have got into the house, like raccoons and possums. Then I'd release them back into the wild."

Without Steven's usual enthusiasm, the discussion that day felt sad and flat. We talked about the ending of "Bartleby," but no one had anything significant to say.

The injury to Bartleby's soul, the narrator learns at the end of the story, happened a long time ago, when, already "by nature and misfortune prone to a pallid hopelessness," he was employed in the Dead Letters Office, charged with sorting out those missives meant "for the flames." This experience had a terrible impact on him—and it's interesting that the next job he chooses, working as a scrivener, involves copying out somebody else's words, communicating with other people while remaining essentially alone.

The sadness of these dead letters is horribly specific. Each is destined for a particular individual, at a very particular time. Their recipients, for the most part, are deceased. These ill-fated transactions seem to have the same effect on Bartleby that the Congo journey has on Marlow in *Heart of Darkness*: they show how communication is an illusion, and how each of us is alone in the universe. Their misery deadens Bartleby's soul, but he's not a victim of a mental disorder or brain disease; on the contrary, he's perfectly lucid, intelligent, and stable. He's simply lost faith in humanity. This is Bartleby's "diagnosis," although it's not a sickness but a particular way of being in the world. And in this choice there seems to lurk, as the narrator observes, "a certain calm disdain." Bartleby isn't in the least unhinged: "Not a wrinkle of agitation gripped him." His mind, like that of Kurtz, is perfectly functional. As the narrator discovers, "it was his soul that suffered, and his soul I could not reach." This is the tragedy of the story: Bartleby is helpless in that he's beyond help—from anyone, including himself.

Most of the men saw the story's ending as a letdown. They'd been expecting something to happen that explained Bartleby's behavior—something more dramatic, that is, than the facts gleaned by the narrator. They complained that the ending didn't make sense. They'd been expecting the time and effort they'd put into reading the story to somehow pay off, to leave them with something, if only a feeling of closure or satisfaction or relief. Now, it was as though Melville—or I, perhaps—had scammed them.

"It was full of loose ends," objected Vincent.

"It didn't add up," protested Donald.

"I was thinking that maybe Bartleby would turn out to be a ghost or something," complained Turk.

Kevin was indignant. "I couldn't get no moral to it," he argued.

I was starting to realize what they expected from literature: a clever point, an enlightening lesson, a key "takeaway." They had little tolerance for indirection, oblique connections, arbitrary sidetracks. In short, they wanted a fast and obvious return on their investment.

I can remember a time when I used to feel the same way. I thought I knew what literature looked like, what it did. I thought it came and grabbed you by the throat and shook you up. If I wasn't grabbed and shaken, I blamed the book. I didn't understand, at the time, there was some literature that crept up on you quietly and gradually, without you even knowing it. These days, when I find myself struggling with a book, I realize the difficulty I'm having is probably due to the fact that, even now, in my late forties, I'm not ready for it yet. It might be a book for a later stage of life. In some ways, the more I read, the more ignorant I feel—and this is just one of the ways in which literature does not, despite the clichés, "make us smarter." When the men complained about having to read books that were "boring" and "irrelevant," I tried to remember how difficult it could be to confront my limitations, to meet my ignorance face-to-face.

I should probably have left "Bartleby" there, but I was still hoping one of the men might have something to say about the story that would help me see it differently. Anyone who's spent a long time in prison must, I thought, have witnessed more than their share of Bartleby-like behavior: refusal, negation, and inertia. I wanted the prisoners to help me understand why, when Bartleby says and does almost nothing, his influence becomes so disturbing and pervasive that everyone around him ends up repeating his pet phrase, acceding to his desires, and indulging his "preferences" in ways they can barely articulate or justify. I made one final venture.

"Anyone ever know a guy like Bartleby?" I asked them.

"I did," said Charles after a moment. "There used to be a guy here called Mike Martin. Some of you guys probably remember him. He was stuck in a wheelchair. They had to push him to the prison hospital every day for medication and treatment and then push him back again. I'd see him there at the clinic: he'd wait around for hours every day for somebody to take him back to his cell. They just forgot about him. He was only fifty when he died, twenty years into a life sentence, no chance of parole. I don't know whether he killed himself or whether he died of neglect, but I think he was like Bartleby. He just preferred not to."

There was a long silence.

"Any other final thoughts about 'Bartleby'?" I asked.

This time, the last word went to Guy. "It was a waste of time," he said. "Nothing happened. He was weird, he went to prison, and he died."

3

HAM ON RYE

Charles Bukowski's *Ham on Rye* had not been on my original agenda—it wasn't a book that was especially important to me—but the men had struggled so much with *Heart of Darkness* and "Bartleby," I felt as though they deserved something they could relate to more closely, and *Ham on Rye* was at least relatively modern and accessible (it was published in 1982). Too, I had a feeling the men might connect with Bukowski's thinly veiled alter ego, Henry Chinaski, a vulnerable and sensitive kid whose difficult childhood forces him to adopt a tough-guy persona.

When reading the novel in the past, I'd been too preoccupied by character and incident to pay much attention to style and technique, but this time I found myself wanting to look behind the scenes to think more about how Bukowski put the story together. *Ham on Rye*, I realized when I reread the novel, is full of tension and suspense. This surprised me. Tension and suspense usually emerge from a solidly structured plot, but the plot of *Ham on Rye* is almost as loose and incidental as the mise-en-scène (it's set in Depression-era Los Angeles, but it could be pretty much anywhere). The anticipation, I realized, is created not by plot but by style. Bukowski's prose is completely fluent and almost transparently accessible, and the narrator's surly cynicism packs a tough punch.

What makes *Ham on Rye* particularly engaging is Henry's total lack of interest in being entertaining. He just tells us what happened. This can be shockingly and unexpectedly funny, and there's something oddly reassuring about the way he never judges or moralizes but just reports what he sees about the people around him and how they live. "It didn't pay to trust another human being," he resolves, after yet another disappointment. He accepts the cruelty and violence in his life without wanting to deny them, or try and improve things, or close his eyes to the darkness, or point a finger in blame. Instead, he learns to handle the bleakness of his existence, and what saves him is alcohol. Drink numbs him into a state where he can meet cruelty with cruelty. "Getting drunk was good," he learns. "I decided that I would always like getting drunk."

MARCH 13, 2013

Our first discussion of *Ham on Rye* took place in a different classroom, one that came to be our regular room for the next year or so. When I arrived, only Guy, Steven, and Sig were there. Unthinkingly, I closed the heavy classroom door behind me. I didn't realize it would lock automatically.

Although I'd inadvertently locked myself in a room with three men who might well be convicted murderers, it didn't occur to me to be scared. I'd been coming into the prison every week for six months now, and I'd grown perfectly comfortable with the setting and the men—Guy, Steven, and Sig in particular. It never crossed my mind that they might have taken the opportunity to harm me, even though it was dark in the room. You'd have thought it was nighttime but for a faint ray of sunlight making its way through the high window, lined with wide green vents. I went to turn on the light, but discovered a protective plate covered the switch.

"Aren't we allowed turn the light on?" I asked Sig.

"No. You need a key," said Sig. "But I know how to jimmy it if you've got a paper clip."

I didn't have a paper clip but I offered him a bobby pin.

"Perfect," said Sig, and expertly flipped the switch. The light came on. Looking back, given the combined height and weight of these three men, I suppose they could have tossed me around like a rag doll; but the truth is, I thought of myself as their partner in crime rather than a potential victim. As Sig and I had been fixing the light switch, Steven had been signaling our predicament to the video monitor in the wall, and eventually the CO came to unlock the door. By now the rest of the men were waiting outside in the hall, along with a man in civilian clothes whom Vincent introduced as the new schoolteacher. His classroom was being used, Vincent said, and he needed somewhere to wait for half an hour or so. He sat awkwardly at a desk at the back of our room while we talked about *Ham on Rye*.

I hadn't had the chance to send the men copies of the book in advance, so we began by reading aloud, the way we'd done with *Heart of Darkness*. This time, however, instead of starting at the beginning, I suggested taking a look at a particular episode in which the young narrator and his friends hitch a ride to an air show where they hide under the bleachers in order to look up a woman's skirt. Before they began reading the book on their own, I wanted the men to get a feel for Bukowski's blunt, stripped-down prose. They read with pleasure, obviously relieved to be reading familiar language for a change. Charles read the last section, with its throwaway final sentence: "I didn't know which was more exciting, the air race, the parachute jump that failed, or the cunt."

"At first, the line seems so straightforward and uninflected, but there's so much going on there," I said.

The prisoners loved it, the last phrase especially—"the cunt"—and enjoyed saying it out loud until Vincent started to get nervous. He was especially conscious of the new teacher in the corner.

"Walls have ears, you guys," he kept muttering frantically. "Keep it down!"

I felt apprehensive, too, but I also couldn't help enjoying the men's enthusiasm. Part of what they liked about the book was the freedom of Bukowski's language. They loved the fact that I'd chosen a book full of what they referred to as "curse words."

"You know, reading curse words in a book and hearing you say them lets us all know it's OK to speak freely," said Charles. "I like that."

Charles, I noticed, was following along closely as each man read, and when we talked about the book's style, he jotted down notes on a legal pad resting on a sort of homemade clipboard. By now I'd understood that although neither *Heart of Darkness* nor "Bartleby" had made much of an impression on him, Charles had read both books closely enough to get emotionally involved with them, even if the emotion in question was begrudging resentment.

For the following week I asked the men to read the first twenty short chapters on their own.

MARCH 20, 2013

"Well, what did you guys make of the first part of *Ham on Rye*?"

"A real book at last." Guy had a big smile on his face, and a big black eye. Steven—the dog, not his friend—had apparently bitten him in the face. So much for the animal's skillful training, I thought.

No doubt, the men were enjoying *Ham on Rye*. The atmosphere was relaxed; the prisoners weren't struggling but chatting naturally and happily, with no need for any of my questions or prompts. They all got a kick out of (and possibly shared) Henry's attitude toward the American public: "A whole god-damned nation of assholes driving automobiles, eating, having babies, doing everything in the worst way possible." They appreciated his observations about life ("Nothing was interesting, nothing") and identified with his worldly cynicism.

In Henry Chinaski, more so than in Marlow or Bartleby, the men could recognize someone whose experiences in life had left him at odds with the human race. This was a subject of particular importance to the men. Most of them felt, unsurprisingly, oppressed by their circumstances. We talked about their own situation, but we also talked about people outside the prison who chose to live in ways that are equally ascetic, cut off not only from the wider world but also from other human beings— isolated not by necessity but by choice. In general, the men felt that however lonely a person might be in prison, there was comfort in the knowledge that everyone around you is in the same boat. Even those serving life sentences acknowledged they were better off at JCI than the homeless addicts and untreated schizophrenics wandering the streets of Baltimore. In prison, however, some certainly had it easier than others. The later in his life a man came to prison, the easier his time there would be. Men who'd lived a full life in the outside world could sustain themselves through their memories, but those without such recollections of a past had little to nourish them.

"Is this book true to life?" asked J.D. at one point. It was one of the first times I'd heard him speak. J.D. was a younger white guy, but he didn't hang out with Guy and Steven. He was closer to Vincent, who'd taken him under his wing. Nonetheless, J.D. still seemed uneasy in the book club, as if he were still unsure if it were the kind of thing he wanted to be involved in.

"Great question. Bukowski described it as semiautobiographical," I said. "Most of the things that happen to Henry in the book also happened to Bukowski, though maybe to a lesser degree. I know Charles Bukowski's father was out of work during the worst years of the Depression, and I know that he was cruel and abusive, like Henry's father in the book."

"That part seemed real," said Sig.

"Did you think so? To me, it seemed a little exaggerated," I said. "I thought Bukowski was playing it up for shock value. Remember that scene where Henry's dad beats him with a razor strop for missing a single blade of grass after he's finished mowing the lawn? Didn't that seem a bit too much to you—a single blade of grass?"

The men disagreed vociferously, recounting similar sadistic tasks set by their own fathers, and the violent punishments imposed when they failed. They all seemed to have had fathers as violent as Henry's, or worse. Kevin recalled how his father would constantly give him black eyes, and broke his bones on more than one occasion.

"There were plenty of times when, if I'd have had a gun, I'd have shot him," Kevin acknowledged. "I've never shot a man, but I've killed a lot of deer and cattle in my life, and I know how to get them in the head with a kill shot. They drop like a ton of bricks. I know it sounds harsh, but there were times when I'd like to have seen that happen to my old man."

"I never felt safe around my dad when he was drinking," admitted Charles. "He'd be calm one minute, and the next he'd be yelling violently about something trivial, like the television being too loud. He'd storm around the house, cursing and threatening my mom. She stayed with him even though he beat her up all the time. That was the reason I lost respect for my mother."

These forays into the personal, I realized, would constantly infiltrate our conversations, and I needed to get used to them and stop worrying about where the discussion was headed. I reminded myself this wasn't a college course, with learning objectives and a syllabus to stick to. We had lots of time to follow digressions; in fact, I soon learned that, as we wandered in and out of the realm of our own experiences, most of what I'd previously seen as digressions weren't actually digressions at all but roundabout ways of getting to something crucial at the heart of the book. In this case, the men's descriptions of domestic violence made me realize that, to them, as to Henry Chinaski (and Charles Bukowski), brutality was a fact of nature.

Every week, when I left the prison, I'd get into my car, put on my headset, and immediately return to the world of whatever audiobook I was currently listening to (usually a nineteenth-century novel). But that day I was distracted. I couldn't get my mind off our conversation about violent fathers. It had disturbed me in a way that wasn't easy to shake off. That evening I'd made plans to go to a bar with my friend Melissa. We wanted to try out different cocktails. We were on a quest to discover our "signature" drinks. Melissa didn't want anything that had too much sugar in it, nor did she want anything with too many artificial ingredients. She liked to keep it natural. I didn't want anything made with whiskey. The smell made me nauseous. We talked about different kinds of liquors and mixers. It was a perfectly ordinary conversation, the kind we have all the time; but on this occasion, after coming straight from the prison, everything felt absurd and indulgent, and I suddenly felt ashamed of myself, sitting there at the bar, clutching a frozen strawberry margarita half the size of my own head. I decided to tell Melissa I was tired and leave early, but as soon as the tequila hit me, the anxiety disappeared and I was able to relax. As Henry Chinaski puts it, "Alcohol makes it easier to accept there's no sense to life."

MARCH 27, 2013

The men finished *Ham on Rye* in record time, and when we'd finished, we watched a movie called *Crazy Love* based loosely on scenes from the book. Although the film wasn't as close to the book as I'd remembered it to be, and although the DVD quality was terrible, and although we had to watch it on an old twenty-inch television, the men found it a real treat and were vocal in their appreciation. In fact, they were vocal all the way through, which didn't detract from their ability to follow the movie, since it was in Flemish with English subtitles. Whenever anything happened that had the slightest hint or promise of sex, they'd all growl or whistle in anticipation, and Guy would slap his thighs and shout, "Awesome!"

In one early scene, the naïve twelve-year-old Henry Chinaski character visits a carnival and musters up the courage to ask a girl if she'd like to ride with him in the tunnel of love. As the ride begins, he sits awkwardly beside her, unsure what to do next.

"Hey, it's you, Vinny," someone said.

I couldn't help smiling. The actor did bear a striking resemblance to the slight, boyish-looking Vincent.

"Yeah," added another joker. "With your sister."

Ham on Rye was pretty explicit in places. Henry Chinaski is frank about his sexual appetite, and as I watched the movie with the convicts, I couldn't help being reminded of the fact that JCI was a men's prison, and every woman who walked through the gates, whatever her age or appearance, was the object of sexual scrutiny. That's just how it was.

When I first started teaching at JCI, this didn't really bother me. It was the winter, and I'd dressed in long sleeves and dark colors, with glasses and my hair tied back. After more than twenty years of college teaching, I'd stopped thinking much about my classroom appearance. My college students were 80 percent female, and it was a long time since I'd been on the radar of the few straight males I taught. Plus, I've always been shy about putting myself forward. Over time, I'd developed a substantial repertoire of psychological armor to deflect attention from myself and toward whatever text we were studying. On top of that I always brought my French bulldog to class—what better diversion?

It was no surprise that those classes or groups run by women at JCI filled up immediately. Some teachers also brought in their undergraduate students, many of whom were attractive young women. The waiting lists for these classes, the men told me half-jokingly, were longer than some of their sentences. The book club also had a long waiting list, although there were only nine places, and with one exception no one dropped out unless they were released or transferred elsewhere. It was around this time that I started to think seriously about the fact that the men who returned to the group week after week—and I set a firm rule that they weren't allowed through the classroom door without home-work in hand—might not have been so keen and dedicated if I'd been a man. I'd noticed they liked to look at me, and the fact made me feel uneasy. I was forty-six when the group began, and it was a long time since guys had looked at me the way they did when I walked across the compound at JCI: as if they were starv-ing and I were a filet mignon. What's more, I knew that a lot of these men were in prison for rape.

To be honest, I was ambivalent about how this made me feel. Every time it happened, I was flooded with conflicting sensations. I was flattered, awkward, proud, embarrassed, self-conscious, ashamed, and self-satisfied. For a while, every time we sat down to talk about *Ham on Rye*, I was aware that, beneath our con-versation, subtle undercurrents were flowing—indecipherable to me—that had nothing to do with the book and everything to do with how I was dressed or the way I was sitting. For once, I had no bulldog to hide behind. It was frustrating. This was exactly how the schoolboy Henry Chinaski and his young pals felt about their English teacher, Miss Gredis, in *Ham on Rye*. "Never had we seen such ankles, such legs, such thighs. . . . And we got to gaze upon her for a full hour each day. There wasn't a boy in that class who wasn't sad when the bell rang ending the English period." I got the sense they talked about me—perhaps even shared their fantasies about me—after class. Like Miss Gredis, no doubt, I wanted the men to be interested not in me but in the books I was trying to introduce them to. After all, one of these days, sooner rather than later, I'd be gone, but the books would remain. If they could transfer their interest from me to the books, I wanted to tell them, they'd be set for life.

But whenever I felt uneasy about this, I'd remind myself of something I know from my own experience: that at its best, learning is erotic. When, as a student, I'd get a crush of my own on a professor, I'd also find myself getting excited about whatever book or poem they were teaching. This happened not only with the male teachers I was attracted to but also with female professors whose looks, lifestyle, or way of being in the world I envied and admired. In the end, it became impossible to separate my love of literature from my romantic fantasies about those figures who, to me, embodied a certain style of living. It's natural to want to emulate the tastes and interests of those you look up to. And it's highly stimulating in all kinds of ways to really get into a deep discussion about literature, especially about books you thought no one else but yourself had ever read. It makes you believe your ideas really matter.

Some of the men, I think, had this experience in the book club: their engagement with my own passion for books enhanced their interest in reading. Others, I think, enjoyed the book club as a way to get off the tier—a pleasant break in an otherwise numbing and predictable routine. And I'm sure there were those who came because they wanted to look at a female body. But whenever I started to suspect one or another of the men of having this as their primary motive, I realized it was impossible to parse and analyze the impulses that drove them. If I was uncertain of my own reasons for coming back to the prison every week, surely the men in the group also had motives that were equally difficult to gauge.

Of all the men, it was Charles who appeared to enjoy *Ham on Rye* the most.

"This is a pretty good book," he said at the end of one of our meetings.

"I'm glad you finally like something we're reading," I said.

"I've been enjoying them all," he said, in his flat, laconic way.

"Honestly?" I was surprised. "You always seem to be sort of annoyed by them."

"Not at all," he said. At the time, I found his disavowal hard to believe.

CHARLES

As a sixty-seven-year-old white guy, Charles seemed to have little connection with the culture of the younger, predominantly

African-American convicts he lived among. Like most of the older men, he preferred having a cell to himself and was irritated when, as sometimes happened, he had to have a cellmate, even a temporary one. He liked silence, he told me; he said it helped him meditate. He didn't have the same need for companionship that most of the younger guys did. He was a loner, and he had a kind of hard-earned wisdom that led the other men to treat him with a respectful distance. Most of the men seemed to dread the long hours they were locked up in their cells, but Charles looked forward to the time he could spend reading, writing, and thinking. I imagined that, were it not regarded as a form of punishment, solitary confinement might be a blessing to him rather than a hardship.

When we look back on our lives, it's tempting to seek out paths, patterns, influential figures, and standout moments of revelation. Most of the men in the book club seemed to feel that in one way or another they had been heading for success until their lives were derailed by the influence of one malignant person or one traumatic event. Something I've learned from literature is that trajectories appear only in retrospect. In the present, all we see are the ordinary ups and downs of everyday affairs. Charles, wiser than most, seemed to have learned this lesson. Whenever he talked about himself, he never talked in terms of a cause-and-effect construction. He understood that life had no shape and no meaning.

Charles had spent most of his life in prison and was now serving a life sentence. Today, his criminal past was long behind him, and it had been years since he'd committed even the most minor infraction. He'd come to terms (as much as possible) with the fact that he was going to die in prison, and had developed a Buddhist practice: he spent time in private meditation every day.

But, unlike the traditional holy man, Charles had renounced the world not because he loved God but because spending his life among criminals had led him to lose faith in humanity. "For the last twenty years or so," he told me when I came to know him better, "I've felt that the fewer people I meet, the fewer people I become acquainted with, the fewer people I talk to, the better off I'll be in the long run." He added, "For me, being in prison is a little like being in a combat zone. I often do an inventory of my physical belongings and get rid of anything I feel I don't really want or need. I like having less things to feel responsible for. I guess I've always lived light and traveled light."

This philosophy was embodied by the gray sweatpants he wore. I came to think of them as a symbol of Charles's independence and self-reliance. He'd customized them with various pockets, buttons, and flaps. When I asked about them, he showed me how they worked. You could undo one set of buttons and remove the two legs, and they turned into shorts for the summer. You could let down a flap here and there, and they became mid-length. There were special pockets to carry particular items, and strings for various other purposes. They were ready for anything. They were almost magical.

"This way," Charles explained to me, "all I ever need is one pair of pants."

Charles had been incarcerated most of his life, in many different prisons. Most recently, before he came to JCI, he'd been a prisoner at Patuxent Institution, a treatment-oriented prison whose staff had included a team of psychiatrists, psychologists, and social workers. Although the prisoners generally agreed that Patuxent had, in the past, been a much better place than JCI, their attitude toward psychology was widely ambivalent. A number of them had told me at various times that although they would never have taken part in therapy of their own accord, the many years of treatment they'd been forced to undergo had helped them understand how their criminal behavior was a form of self-sabotage that could be transformed or outgrown. Still, all in all, they were deeply mistrustful of "headshrinkers." Sometimes they made fun of them, boasting about how easy they were to fool; at other times they had an almost superstitious fear of psychiatrists and psychologists, crediting them with a mind reader's power to identify and interpret their thoughts. While none of them wanted to look like a "mental health case," many of them readily admitted they carried a lot of baggage "up there." Mostly, however, what they despised about shrinks was their power to pry secrets out of people—secrets that would later be used against them, sometimes in court. The psychologists at JCI got death threats from prisoners all the time.

At Patuxent, Charles went through enough psychological evaluation, therapy, treatment, and counseling for the board of review to approve him for leave status in 1986. This meant that if he had a friend or family member in Maryland willing to sponsor and accommodate him, he could leave the prison for occasional weekend furloughs. But Charles's mother and sister both lived out of state, and all his other friends and family members were either dead or estranged from him. So he started looking around for someone who might eventually be willing to sponsor him for a furlough.

A few weeks later, when Charles was in the hospital recovering from a back operation, his mother sent him a magazine in which she'd underlined a classified ad from a Baltimore lady around Charles's age who was looking for pen pals. Charles wrote her a letter and she replied. She had an unusual name. It was pronounced "Norma Lee," but it was written as a single word with only one *e*: Normale.

Charles and Normale wrote back and forth until he felt comfortable enough to ask her about sponsoring and accommodating him on furlough, and she agreed. They met, grew close, and, in time, fell in love. They married at Patuxent Institution on June 8, 1991, and when Normale retired from her career in the Social Security Administration, she moved to Columbia, Maryland, to be closer to Patuxent and to her church. She speaks on the phone to Charles every day (unless the jail is on lockdown or the phones aren't working) and visits him eight times a month, which is the maximum number of visits allowed.

Normale's parents are dead and she doesn't have any children; nonetheless, she's the epicenter of a close-knit community that includes her brothers and sisters-in-law, nephews, great-nieces, a goddaughter, and dozens of friends from the Kittamaqundi Community Church in Columbia. She's an activist on behalf of the homeless, she's survived cancer twice, she volunteers for many different charities, she works at a summer camp for underprivileged girls, she cares for her friends' and neighbors' dogs when their owners are out of town, and she officiates at pet memorial services. On the telephone and in her regular visits, she shares this busy life with Charles. "Normale taught me what love really means," he told me once.

As someone who'd chosen to distance himself from his fellow prisoners, it came as no surprise to me that Charles sympathized with Henry Chinaski's gloomy conclusion about the human race: "I've got to live with these fuckers for the rest of my life." But there's a turning point for Henry, and it comes when he discovers the Los Angeles City Library. When he starts reading, he begins to realize that "words were things that could make your mind hum. If you read them and let yourself feel the magic, you could live without pain, with hope, no matter what happened to you."

Charles had underlined the passage. "Reading is the one thing that makes me feel more alive," he said. "It's the only way to get out of here since they stopped letting us out on work release. When you're reading a good book, you can leave prison for a while, at least in your head."

The day we finished *Ham on Rye*, Charles left the school at the same time as my escort came to pick me up, and he accompanied us down the hall. I noticed he walked stiffly, with a limp. He had a pinched nerve in his back, he told me, from which he'd been suffering for years. It was especially bad after he'd been sitting down for a long time.

We crossed the compound in silence until we came to the fence where we had to go our different ways. The CO who was escorting me stopped to speak to a fellow officer, leaving Charles and me a few moments to chat.

"How long do you think you'll carry on with this book club?" asked Charles.

"I don't know," I said. "I might take a break over the summer, but if I do, I'll probably come back in the fall."

"That's good," he said. "You know, before you came, I was just vegetating, sort of like a potted plant."

"I'm pleased you're enjoying it," I said.

"I'd take any course you were offering, even if it was basket weaving," he said. Then he gave me a brief wave and walked off toward E block, alone.

4

JUNKIE

When I first got to college, the excitement of my new independence led me to experiment with a new self-image. Before long, I'd settled on a punk-goth look. This involved a beaten-up black motorcycle jacket worn over a sweater with the collar and sleeves torn off, a skirt ripped to mid-thigh, fishnet tights, eight-hole Doc Martens boots, and dirty white lace gloves with the fingers cut off. My hair, crimped to death, was part blonde, part pink. It was 1986, the year of *Sid and Nancy*, and I was nineteen. My gutter chic was seriously out of place in Oxford's cloisters and croquet lawns, which was precisely the point. I was secretly flattered when one afternoon, on arriving at an English faculty get-together, I was handed a glass of wine by my tutor, who announced, "I'm sorry, my dear, we don't have any syringes."

Although I liked to play Lou Reed's "Heroin" at high volume, frightening the girls in my dorm, I knew next to nothing about drugs. My friends smoked pot, but whenever I tried it, it made me feel sick and dizzy. I found the taste of alcohol nauseating, although I liked Bulmers cider, which contains five teaspoons of sugar per pint, because it tasted like pop. It was very strong and I'd throw up if I drank more than three pints.

I wanted people to think I was hard and tough, but the punk rock style favored by my friends and I was all naïve bravado. Our leader in matters of taste was my boyfriend Eric. Although he was only three years my senior, Eric was a lifetime ahead in experience. He'd spent his year abroad living above a brothel in Barcelona, and he introduced us to the work of Charles Baudelaire, the Marquis de Sade, and Jean Genet. My friends and I loved to read about criminals, addicts, and thieves. Our touchstone was William S. Burroughs's *Junkie* (originally with the subtitle: *Confessions of an Unredeemed Drug Addict*). We venerated our tattered copy, passing it from hand to hand and appropriating its colorful jargon.

I knew literature didn't always have to focus on rich people, or even the middle classes—I'd encountered the noble poor in Dickens, George Eliot, and Thomas Hardy, and I'd read about the not-so-noble poor in George Orwell and H. G. Wells—but until then I'd never read literature that involved the kind of people Burroughs writes about in *Junkie*. Horror was my cup of tea, but I only knew the kind of horror that elevates ordinary nastiness, making it lofty and supernatural. *Junkie* does just the opposite, grinding your face in the dirt. I chose it for the prisoners to read because I thought they'd be curious about Burroughs's realistic, unflinching description of the addict's underworld. For many of them, this was their domain, or it had been at one time, and I was curious whether they'd recognize themselves in its denizens.

APRIL 10, 2013

I handed out copies of *Junkie*, gave the men some information about Burroughs and his life, and all at once, before we'd even begun to read the book, we were in the middle of a frank discussion about drugs. The book's author and narrator, Bill Lee—the pseudonym used by Burroughs when the book was first published—claims that, to get addicted, you've got to be determined. "It took me almost six months to get my first habit, and then the withdrawal symptoms were mild," he says. "I think it no exaggeration to say it takes about a year and several hundred injections to make an addict." The prisoners all disagreed with Burroughs on this point, but they liked the way his claim opposed the dogma of the twelve-step groups popular in prison like Narcotics Anonymous, with their unshakable premises, their uncontestable assertion that all drugs are the same, and you're either an addict or in recovery.

The men in the group who'd been drug users thought this version of addiction was simple, even infantilizing. In contrast, they were pleased to learn that Burroughs, despite his drug use, lived a long life, continuing to write and paint into his eighties. In his prologue to the 1953 edition of *Junkie*, Carl Solomon calls Burroughs "an unrepentant drug addict." He often kicked his habit, sometimes for years at a time, but always knew he'd use again when the time came. The men agreed that you could live your whole life this way—it's how many of them lived themselves—but in NA the only goal was "complete and continuous abstinence." There was no place for the "unrepentant."

One man confessed that his first time using heroin had been the turning point in his life.

"It was like, I don't know, like finding this . . . this magic

thing," he said, his eyes shining. It was what I'd always been looking for. When I'm on H it's, like . . . this pure version of myself.
It's who I really am inside."

"You sound unrepentant," I observed.

"Damn straight," he affirmed. "Truth is, long as H exists in
the world, I'm gonna use it."

"Do you miss it?"

"Are you kidding me?" He gave a brief, contemptuous laugh.
"You can get anything you want in here. I've got so many added
years for dirty urine, it's like a whole 'nother bit."

Of course, you could get anything in prison. Deprivation creates desire, and desire creates demand. Every so often the men
would be required to take urine tests, sometimes in their cells
and sometimes in an area near the visiting room. Prisoners
called to take these tests were supposedly selected at random by
a computer, but the men believed the COs had "snitch lists" or
picked out prisoners based on their suspicious behavior, or just
for no reason at all. Some of the men, I felt, regarded the Department of Corrections as their adversary in an ongoing game, the
object of which was to score as often and in whatever form they
could. In this way, their lives gained a kind of meaning from
pursuit itself, whether of coffee, cigarettes, or products more il-
licit and more difficult to obtain. Perhaps this is what Burroughs
means when he writes, "Junk is not a kick. It is a way of life."

Most of the former addicts admitted they'd started to use
when they were bored and directionless teenagers looking for
anything to give them a new high. According to Burroughs,
"You become a narcotics addict because you do not have strong
motivations in any other direction." When asked by an inter-
viewer why he felt compelled to record the experiences he describes in *Junkie*, Burroughs replied, "I didn't feel compelled. I

had nothing else to do. Writing gave me something to do every day. I don't feel the results were at all spectacular. *Junkie* is not much of a book, actually. I knew very little about writing at that time."

I grew up around people who used drugs, and for me the motivation in the other direction was reading. "Books always absorbed me more than anything else," I told the men. "Even now I'll sometimes pour myself a cocktail and settle down with a book. A couple of hours later, when I put the book down and get up to go to bed, I'll notice the drink still sitting there."

The men were unconvinced.

"I got to say, I read a few books, and I can't imagine any being *that* good," said Kevin.

Later, as I was leaving the prison and walking back to my car, I realized that one of the reasons I liked being at JCI was that the prison absorbed me in the same way I'd get absorbed in a book. Deep in the world of the prisoners, I'd be temporarily out of touch with my own life. Every time I left the prison and got to the parking lot, my own world would start coming back to me, piece by piece. Back in the wider world of friends, plans, work, and responsibilities, sometimes I didn't think about the men again until my next trip to the prison. But as soon as I entered its gates, I'd leave my own life behind and return to theirs.

APRIL 17, 2013

For a while, I'd noticed that Guy and Steven hadn't been on speaking terms. Now they were friendly again, although they weren't sitting together—which worried me, for Guy's sake. I thought of him as childlike and vulnerable. He'd once told me he was an orphan. He had a brother somewhere, but the only person who came to visit him regularly was an aunt. I was surprised to learn he was twenty-eight, a few years older than Steven, who seemed by far the more balanced of the two. Physically, Guy looked like an overgrown kid, so tall and skinny that his standard-issue prison jeans were always hanging halfway down his backside in gangsta fashion, revealing his oversized underpants. Like Steven, he could be animated and enthusiastic, but he didn't have his friend's intelligence or constitutional optimism, and could fall into fits of inattentive petulance, slouching down in his chair or slumping forward over his tray table with his head on his arms. He was impulsive and impressionable, and could seem naïve and unworldly, with an unguarded interest in things he knew nothing about. He'd often ask me about England, which in Guy's mind seemed to be a place you visited in a time machine. He wanted to know if it was true, for instance, that the clock face of Big Ben had a hole in the middle through which aristocrats would dump the contents of their chamber pots on the peasants.

One day something I said reminded him that he had a question for me. Reaching into the pocket of his sagging jeans, he pulled out a torn scrap of paper.

"Who's Guy Fawkes?" he asked me.

"He tried to blow up the House of Lords back in the seventeenth century. He led a group of rebels who planned what they called the Gunpowder Plot. They stockpiled barrels of gunpowder underneath the House of Lords, but the plot was discovered just in time. Why do you ask?"

"I saw this calendar, and on the fifth of November it said 'Guy Fawkes Night.'"

"The fifth of November is when the plot was discovered. In England, we build fires and have fireworks to celebrate."

"But you said the plot got discovered, right?"

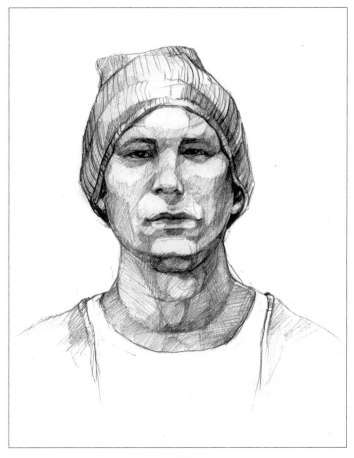

GUY

"Right."

"So why do people celebrate him?"

"They celebrate the fact that the plot was discovered and the House of Lords wasn't blown up."

"So people didn't want it to work?"

"Well, no."

"They didn't want to blow up all the lords?"

"That's right."

"How come?"

"Well, because they ruled the country."

"But Guy Fawkes must have been a pretty cool dude, right?"

"In some ways, I suppose."

"And his name, you say it like mine, *Guy*, right? Not like the French way"—he sneered—"*Gee*."

"That's right."

Guy put the scrap of paper back in his pocket and swung back in his chair, grinning as happily as if he'd just found out he was the son of a duke.

Like Steven, Guy was a short-timer. I don't know why he'd been put among the lifers at JCI, but he was expecting to be paroled any day. He'd served four years of an eight-year sentence for drug dealing—a sentence that took into account his prior convictions: theft, the possession of a firearm with a felony conviction, and burglary in the second degree. I found it difficult to imagine this lazy kid as a violent criminal, although he was definitely excitable, and he certainly had a limited attention span. Often, after half an hour of class, he'd rest his head on his folded arms and nod off.

For now, he was alone in this. Even if they didn't particularly like the story or style, the other men all seemed interested in Burroughs's descriptions of the guns he'd owned, his accounts of robbing drunks on the New York subway and weaseling morphine scripts out of "croakers." They were also curious about the kinds of drugs used by Burroughs and his underworld cronies (mainly morphine, heroin, Pantopon, Dilaudid, codeine), and how much they cost. They enjoyed Burroughs's graphic picture of the physical horrors of drug addiction (uremic poisoning, chronic constipation) and debated the advantages of his various remedies. Burroughs always preferred the incremental "Chinese cure," a gradual weaning that involved replacing the drug with increasing doses of "Wampole's Tonic." In *Junkie*, he alternates the "Chinese cure" with trips to the U.S. Narcotics Farm in Kentucky, a place where men with drug addictions could voluntarily admit themselves for experimental treatments.

As I left the prison each week, a mass of blue-shirted men would begin crowding toward the chow hall for the first dinner shift. The prisoners came to know the rhythms and dictates of incarceration at a bodily level, and they weren't alone. Every day, as dinnertime drew near, the resident flock of geese began gathering by the dining hall, pigeons lined the roof of the buildings, and seagulls settled around the Dumpsters. Semi-feral cats emerged from behind the buildings and under the fences, part of a posse that spent its time, like the gulls, between the prison and the nearby fish market just over a mile away.

APRIL 24, 2013

The following week, we were deep in the middle of our discussion about *Junkie* when J.D. arrived late. J.D. had a Caesar haircut, a cobweb tattooed on his right elbow, and enormous arm muscles, although his legs seemed to be of ordinary size. Maybe he was planning to work on them next. Today, he was also wearing a pair of thick-lensed, black-framed glasses. They gave his face an intellectual expression that made an odd mismatch with his muscular tattooed body.

"Looking smart today, J.D.," I said as he pulled up a chair. "I didn't know you wore glasses."

"I don't. I hate them," he grimaced. "I had to wear them. I just got back from court."

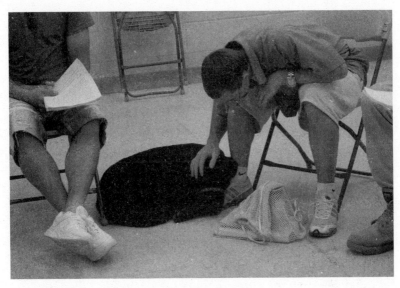

J.D.

"Oh?"

"Yeah. I'm trying to get my sentence reduced."

I'd read about J.D.'s case. It was a tragic one. An only child, he'd quit school after tenth grade and worked full-time to help support his parents. He lived deep in the country, not far from the Delaware state border, with his mother and his grandfather. J.D.'s girlfriend had broken up with him when he was nineteen, and J.D. got caught up in a feud with her new boyfriend. One September evening, after nine months of provocation, J.D. recognized his rival's pickup truck shining its headlights into his home, and he snapped. He'd been drinking, and he was, as he put it later, "at the end of my rope." He grabbed his rifle, ran outside, and fired three shots at the pickup truck. The first two shots hit the body of the vehicle, and the third hit the bed of the truck—where, unbeknownst to J.D., a fourteen-year-old boy had been riding. The child was killed instantly.

J.D. had received a life sentence for first-degree murder. He'd served nine and a half years when I met him, five of them at JCI. Now his attorney was trying to get the judge to renegotiate his sentence on the grounds of his good behavior over the last ten years.

"How did it go?" I asked.

"It went very well," said J.D. firmly.

"So? What did you get?"

"Fifty years," he said.

If that was good news, I wondered, what would bad news have been? Yet J.D. seemed genuinely thrilled by the outcome. Perhaps, over his ten years in prison, he'd learned to be grateful for small mercies.

"Did you prepare a speech for court?" Vincent asked him.

"I was going to, but then I thought it wouldn't sound sincere if I just read something off a piece of paper," J.D. told him. "I thought it would be better to just say whatever came into my mind when I met the victim's family. But I was under so much pressure, I lost my nerve. I didn't know what to say."

"Yeah. That public speaking is a motherfucker," agreed Donald, a man I could not imagine losing his nerve. I could picture him being intimidating, but never tongue-tied.

"I'm going to appeal again, though," said J.D. "Maybe we can get it down to forty. Though I'd ask for the death penalty if I could. You know, an eye for an eye."

I'd always found J.D. hard to read. He was a practicing Christian, and I first got to know him in my writing class, in which he wrote a surprisingly charming paper about elephants. "This story is about one of God's most beautiful and intelligent creatures, the elephant," it began. "It is my favorite animal, and I will be telling you why." It was my first glimpse of J.D.'s boyish, sentimental side, which elicited regular teasing among the men. They made fun of him for getting tearful (though he denied the charge) when, after three months of training, it was time for him to say good-bye to his first service dog, Savoy.

"It's not true. I wasn't crying," J.D. had protested. "I didn't even go when they came to take him away."

I didn't see why J.D. was being so defensive about his attachment to Savoy, although I suppose there's something to be said for holding back your tears when you live among tough guys. Maybe the men were trying to get him to harden up.

Another time, he wrote a paper about his girlfriend. "I feel truly blessed," he wrote, "that early in my life I have found the person that I became one flesh with, and I hope to be released soon to spend the rest of my days with my other half." I was surprised, then—given J.D.'s Christian values—when I learned his "other half" was actually married to somebody else.

"How do you manage to spend so much time on the phone with your girlfriend without her husband getting suspicious?" I asked him one day.

"He drives a truck," said J.D. "He's always on the road."

"Doesn't he check the phone bill?"

"She's got unlimited minutes."

"You really think she's going to break up with him?"

"Well, I've got some ideas," he said. "Her husband doesn't like fat girls, so for a while I was trying to persuade her to get fat so he'd divorce her. But she says he won't divorce her no matter how fat she gets, so now I've got to think of something else."

Sometimes J.D. could be dark and sullen, and whenever he was in a mood like this, the other men always joked that "Sport Coat" was in town. "Sport Coat" was prison slang for the guy who moves in on your girl when you're away—though as Charles pointed out, if anybody was "Sport Coat" in this situation, it was J.D.

J.D. didn't think much of *Junkie*. He told me he subscribed to *National Geographic* and liked to read things that were "informative" and "taught you something." Personally, I thought *Junkie* served these functions, but obviously J.D. felt differently.

I'd always found *Junkie* a very dark book, but when I'd used it in college classes, my students always found it a breeze. They never considered it scary or disturbing, and many of them told me they found it "an easy read." I even remember one girl saying that, after finishing *Junkie*, she'd lent it to her mother, because "she loves that kind of thing." For whatever reason—and perhaps they just weren't reading closely—my students weren't at all fazed by the book's sleaziest scenes, like that in which Burroughs goes cold turkey in a prison cell. Here, his shattered body, "raw, twitching, tumescent," lying on a bench, "junk-frozen-flesh in agonizing thaw," suddenly comes to life when he falls to the floor and the sudden rush of blood to his genitals causes sparks to explode behind his eyes: "the orgasm of a hanged man when the neck snaps."

Reading *Junkie* with the prisoners made it seem darker than ever. I was especially struck, this time, by a character named Bill Gains, the son of a bank president, whose "routine" is "stealing overcoats out of restaurants." "He was not merely negative," writes Burroughs. "He was positively invisible; a vague respectable presence. There is a certain kind of ghost that can only materialize with the aid of a sheet or other piece of cloth to give it outline. Gains was like that. He materialized in someone else's overcoat." Bill Gains seems to be the literal version of a state of mind, a symbolic representation of the pleasure we get from another person's misery. The worst kind of junk pusher, Gains smiles as he reports on other people's misfortunes, getting a special kick out of seeing nonusers develop a habit.

Through his portrayal of men like Bill Gains (and *Junkie* is full of them), Burroughs shows us that caring for each other is not, as most people like to believe, hardwired into our species. It turns out that we're not naturally social animals. In the junk world, there's no redemption ever, even in old age, even at the end. Signs of weakness are met with violence. You get older, and things just get worse. At the same time you get used to them. There's no forgiveness, no place for judgments or opinions, just suffering, struggling human beings. Like *Ham on Rye*, *Junkie* is unrelentingly honest. What makes these addicts' behavior seem so crazy to us is just the situation they're in. We may not be in their place, but if we were, we may very well act that way too.

But to the prisoners the book was getting "depressing."

"*Of course* it's depressing," I said, "but that's what makes it so powerful. You've got to give it time. If you concentrate, you can get curious about what *makes* it depressing, and that's really interesting. You can get engrossed in it. You need that 'motivation in the other direction'—one of those things Burroughs says can lead you away from junk."

What I really wanted to say to them was this: if you pay attention and keep working at it, eventually your eyes will adjust to the darkness, and everything that lives there will be illuminated for you the way things suddenly come into focus when a ray of sunlight breaks into a dark room. You've got to keep trying and trying, going back again and again until it grips you, until the world of these addicts starts to seem as meaningful a world as your own. You can't just give up as soon as it starts to get difficult and uncomfortable. That just means you've got to concentrate, try harder, dig in further, work out what's going on—both in the book and in your head.

I wanted to say it but I didn't. Everything that day was patchy and disconnected. We kept getting interrupted. Some men turned up late; others left early. People would stick their heads in the room to say hello to their pals, disrupting the discussion. Charles had to leave to go to the commissary. Turk was called to the visiting room. J.D. was in one of his sullen moods ("Sport Coat" was in town). Guy wasn't there; in fact, I didn't see him again for six months. He'd been sent to the lockup. Men were sent to the lockup for all kinds of reasons—sometimes they themselves were never told why—but from overhearing the men's conversation I learned that Guy had been using drugs. I thought of his moodiness, his slumping down in his seat, his nodding off during the discussion. The whole time we'd been reading *Junkie*, I realized, he'd been high.

In *Junkie*, Burroughs compares the intense discomfort of withdrawal to the transition from plant back to animal, "from a painless, sexless, timeless state back to sex and pain and time, from death back to life." While Burroughs can and does stay sober for many months at a time, he always goes back to junk, and in the end you realize that junk will always win out because however awful the nightmare of addiction might be, it's preferable to the unchanging, desperate boredom of ordinary life. As Burroughs says, you need strong motivations in another direction to resist the pull of junk, and it was hard to imagine Guy being motivated by anything much at all.

How stupid I had been. *Junkie* contained vivid descriptions of heroin intoxication. I was worried that, by asking him to read the book, I'd played a part in Guy's relapse.

"We shouldn't have been reading *Junkie*," I realized. "That must have been what sent Guy back to doing drugs."

Someone snorted with laughter. Guy, the men told me, didn't go *back* to doing drugs: he'd been high since he first got to prison. And *Junkie* had nothing to do with it. No one had seen him so much as open the cover. Now I felt even more foolish. Here I was, claiming literature can give you a reason not to use drugs, then assuming Guy had relapsed and it was literature that had caused it. Literature had nothing to do with it. Drugs can be bought in prison just as they can on the streets, and the boredom and monotony of life behind bars must surely increase the temptation to use.

There are no "dealers" in prison, I learned. Different men get hold of drugs at various times in different ways, and sources change from week to week (if anyone sold them consistently for several days in a row, they'd soon be found out). Some are smuggled in as contraband; some prisoners sell their prescription medications, certain of which could apparently be crushed into a powder and snorted for a quick high. Six hundred milligrams of Neurontin or 75 milligrams of Wellbutrin could be bought for a postage stamp. Guy, I learned, had been using Suboxone, a heroin substitute. His black eye, which he'd blamed on Steven the dog, had actually been the result of an unpaid drug debt. Looking back, it should have been obvious to me—how could a well-trained service dog give his handler a black eye?—but, too busy trying to stimulate the men's interest in *Junkie*, I'd failed to notice the presence, right in front of my eyes, of a sleepy, nodding drug addict.

MAY 1, 2013

The cinder-block classroom felt like the inside of an oven. The heat was almost unbearable. I wore a cap-sleeved T-shirt, and to my great annoyance I was turned away at the front gate because "you can't wear sleeveless." I got back in my car, drove to the nearby strip mall, grabbed a long-sleeved T-shirt from the Goodwill store—it happened to be Day-Glo pink—and rushed back to the prison. The guys gave me a round of applause when I got to the classroom; still, much of our time had already been lost, and the men didn't seem to have any interest in discussing *Junkie*. My T-shirt was too much of a distraction. It hurt their eyes, they said.

"What's going on?" I asked them. "I thought you all liked this book."

I noticed Kevin and Sig exchange a look. Finally, Kevin spoke up.

"Yeah, so this guy, whatever his name is. OK, he was married when the book started. What happened to his wife and kids? Seems like he's turned queer."

"Good point. He *was* queer. In fact, he wrote a book called *Queer*. It's the companion volume to *Junkie*. As a matter of fact, I was thinking of asking you to read it next."

"You've got to be kidding me!" exclaimed Kevin. "Nobody in his right mind would walk around prison carrying a book called *Queer*."

In the book's earlier chapters, the men hadn't enjoyed reading about characters they found despicable—men like Roy the lush worker or Doolie the rat—but these individuals are incidental to Burroughs's narrative. When they learned that Burroughs himself, despite his marriage, was a self-confessed "queer," most of them turned away from *Junkie*, and I was confused and frustrated by their attitude. Later I learned that in the last ten years, JCI had become far more homophobic than it had ever been in the past, when openly gay couples had been commonplace. These days they kept to themselves. Long-timers speculated that the change was caused by the introduction of female COs. These women, rather than other men, were now the primary focus of the prisoners' sexual attention, even though CO/prisoner relationships were strictly against the rules.

There were no conjugal visits at JCI, and when their wives or girlfriends came to see them, convicts were allowed only a hug when they arrived and another before they left. (Guards stood in the visiting room watching closely to be sure no extra affection was expressed.) Surely there had to be plenty of men at JCI in homosexual relationships. I guessed these were "on the down low." I wondered whether the most aggressively homophobic men might even be in such relationships themselves. This was especially ironic, I thought, since part of the punishment inherent in the prison system is the way it abolishes the boundary between public and private. Prisoners aren't supposed to have any secrets. Everything is supposed to be open and transparent. Private tastes and preferences are a luxury of the free.

What particularly depressed me, however, was the prisoners' apparent inability to imagine people like Roy, Doolie, and Bill having inner lives like their own, tormented by denial and desire. Even more frustrating was the men's failure to realize that the way they saw the thugs and thieves in *Junkie* was how most people on the outside saw *them*. Although I didn't say so, I'd chosen *Junkie* because—on the surface at least—it takes as its subject the sordid concerns of a bunch of criminal types who can't imagine solutions to their problems other than violence. Burroughs shows us, nevertheless, that a limited verbal and even intellectual capacity doesn't necessarily reflect a diminished inner life, and that social deprivation has no effect on sensitivity to emotional pain. One of the things *Junkie* reveals is that people never stop struggling and suffering, that lives advance and grow even in the dark, that every history has its personal course. But instead of accepting these fellow victims and recognizing their claim to kinship, the prisoners saw them as unworthy of their time. I thought again of the narrator's words in "Bartleby": "So true it is, and so terrible too, that up to a certain point the thought or sight of misery enlists our best affections; but, in certain special cases, beyond that point it does not."

It wasn't only the men's failure to engage with Burroughs that depressed me. There was something else as well. Our discussion about *Junkie* had reminded me of a moment in Graham Greene's novel *The End of the Affair* when the protagonist, an author, suddenly realizes that his writing is "as unimportant a drug as cigarettes to get one through the weeks and years." Talking to the men about books had made me see very clearly that, for most of the prisoners, reading was just a way of passing time. It wasn't as expensive or damaging to their physical health as cigarettes or Suboxone would have been but, in the end, perhaps it was just as futile, and without the high.

5

ON THE YARD

After we'd finished *Junkie*, I took a break from the book club and taught another writing class. There were so many men in the prison who wanted to join the college program, and so few classes offered, that I felt guilty limiting the book club to the same nine men. On the other hand, I knew that making it any larger would mean it would be impossible to have coherent discussions, so I eased my conscience by taking breaks now and then to teach larger, more traditional kinds of classes.

The men in the book club kept asking me when we were going to reconvene (in November, I promised), and they asked me if we could read a prison novel next. I read a lot of prison writing that summer and fall, looking for a book that evoked the peculiar everydayness of life inside. My partner David, a movie critic, suggested I look at *On the Yard*—he'd interviewed the author, Malcolm Braly, in 1978, when the movie adaptation had come out—and as soon as I started reading it, I knew I'd found the right one. Braly, who spent almost twenty years in various prisons for burglary, wrote *On the Yard* toward the end of his stretch in San Quentin, although prison authorities threatened to revoke his parole when they learned about it, and he had to finish writing it in secret. The novel finally came out in 1967, when the author's parole had expired.

It was a long time since I'd been so deeply involved in a work of fiction. When I wasn't reading the book, I was worrying in the back of my mind about what would happen to its sympathetic protagonist, Paul Juleson, a thoughtful man who's wracked with guilt after murdering his wife in a moment of jealous rage. Juleson manages to get into debt to Chilly Willy (real name: William Oberholster), a charismatic, twenty-five-year-old thug who rules the prison yard with the help of his two ghoulish henchmen, Gasolino and Society Red. Everything about the book was realistic, although the story was far more exciting and unpredictable than prison life at JCI. (By this time, I'd realized that prisons in fiction have to be volatile and action-packed; you couldn't make a page-turner out of the monotony of real life behind bars.)

NOVEMBER 7, 2013

I'd mailed copies of *On the Yard* to the prison librarian, with a note asking her to instruct the men in the book club to read the first six chapters in advance. When we met, I was pleased to find they seemed to be as gripped by the book as I'd been. They'd also noticed a lot of things I hadn't, like the fact that at first there's no obvious protagonist in *On the Yard*: the narrative focus shifts almost imperceptibly from one point of view to another as we follow a group of convicts from their arraignment through their sentencing. That I hadn't observed the narrative's shifting viewpoint made me realize how subtle and well crafted Braly's writing is. He takes what in everyday experience seems inconsequential (or chaotic, or both) and, almost invisibly, makes order out of it.

The convicts in *On the Yard* are a mixed bag. Most of them have done time before, some are career criminals, and one or two are going inside for the first time. As always, in their response to the book, the men were practical and realistic. They wondered how each of the characters would get by in prison based on things like the crimes they'd committed, the amount of money they had, what they looked like, and how experienced they were.

Sig kicked off the discussion. "I like these characters. They're three-dimensional. You don't get that in a lot of books about criminals. You might not like these guys, but you can understand their motives."

"I know. That's one of the things I enjoy most about this book," I said. "I love how Braly gets under each character's skin and shows us what drives him."

"Right," agreed Sig. "Some are smart, some are dumb, some are violent, some are perverts. There are no stereotyped criminals. They're all different. Just like us."

One thing I'd wondered about when reading the book was whether the scheme of relationships in most prisons is really as clear and systematic as it is in *On the Yard*, where there's a very obvious set of rules that determine the connections between prisoners, guards, and institutional authorities. Although the prison isn't named, *On the Yard* is clearly set in San Quentin, where the traditions have been inherited from earlier generations. I wondered whether, at prisons with a shorter history, like JCI, the rules were equally obvious.

The men were divided on this question.

"There's no convict codes here anymore," asserted Charles. "Twenty or thirty years ago, things used to be different. Now there are cliques, gangs, and religious groups. That's where the rules and codes of conduct come from now. People who keep to themselves and aren't in any of the groups or gangs often get mistreated unless they manage to win people's respect."

Vincent disagreed. "Sure there are convict codes. What about everything that just went down with the BGF?"

"That's a gang," protested Charles.

"Gangs have convict codes," countered Vincent.

"Wait . . . what's the BGF? What just went down?" I was lost. The men went on to tell me about thirteen female COs at the Baltimore City Detention Center who'd recently been indicted for smuggling drugs and cell phones into the prison in their underwear, shoes, and hair to help the BGF (Black Guerrilla Family) run their narcotics ring from jail.*

"So all the COs were members of the BGF?" I asked.

"Possibly," said Vincent. "They might have got jobs in the detention center so they could help the gang. Or maybe they wanted to join the BGF and this was their initiation ritual. Four of them were pregnant by Bulldog White, the BGF leader. Two of them had tattoos of his name, one on her wrist and one on her neck."

---

* I learned the rest of the details from an article on the BGF scandal in the *New Yorker* by Jeffrey Toobin, "This Is My Jail" (April 14, 2014). In July 2015, Maryland's recently elected Republican governor, Larry Hogan, announced the immediate closure of the Baltimore City Detention Center.

It was hard to believe. The BGF scandal reminded me of certain incidents in *On the Yard*—like Gasolino committing suicide by drinking the contents of a fire extinguisher—in that it was at the same time plausible and totally absurd. The men told me there was nothing new about having COs bring in contraband for prisoners; what was new about this particular affair was that so many officers in the same jail were involved in the same gang. The BGF had obviously taken over the detention center. Everyone found it ironic that none of the high-level wardens and security employees had any idea what was going on in "their" prison.

The BGF setup also reminded me of Chekhov's "Ward No. 6," a story I'd been considering for the book club. In this long tale, the director of a provincial lunatic asylum becomes a prisoner there. The story reveals that those who deal with the incarcerated—if they do so for long enough—eventually begin to resemble those they oversee. It suggests, too, that as in the BGF affair, the public is the mirror of the private, and vice versa. In the persona of Bulldog White, king and convict are two sides of the same coin.

When I looked the case up online, I realized the BGF arrests had caused a huge scandal. People outside the prison system found it impossible to understand how a prison could be infiltrated and governed by members of a criminal gang. The prisoners told me it was almost impossible for people "uptown" (as they called the outside world) to understand the things that happened in prison, from brutal violence to ordinary everyday indignities.

"Yeah. That really came home to me when I was trying to explain to my dad why I got sent to the lockup for something I hadn't done," recalled Steven. "And my dad was, like, 'I think you should go and report it to someone in authority.' I didn't even know how to begin to explain to him that things didn't work that way. That was the last time I tried asking him for advice."

Some of their reluctance to talk was deliberate. It was axiomatic that you shouldn't burden your friends and families with depressing stories, and you had to keep a positive attitude if you wanted your visitors to come back. Oscar Wilde, I remembered, expressed the same sentiment in his essay from prison, *De Profundis*. When his friends visited him, wrote Wilde, "I tried to be as cheerful as possible, and to show my cheerfulness, in order to make them some slight return for their trouble in coming all the way from town to see me. It is only a slight return, I know, but it is the one, I feel certain, that pleases them most."

Yet the men also felt that the kinds of things they'd experienced over the years couldn't be adequately put into words. The same is true of Marlow in *Heart of Darkness*, who, although he's not much of a storyteller (or so he claims), seems somehow compelled to share his experiences in the Congo with his listeners—or at least to make the attempt. The more deeply he gets involved in his narrative, however, the more difficult he finds it to express himself. He curses the fact that he seems condemned to keep on trying to express the ineffable to those who'll never understand. "This is the worst of trying to tell . . . ," he cries. "You can't understand? How could you—with solid pavement under your feet, surrounded by kind neighbors ready to cheer you or to fall on you, stepping delicately between the butcher and the policeman . . ." How, wonders Marlow, can he explain to his listeners—men who live in "holy terror of scandal and gallows and lunatic asylums"—the unspeakable horrors he's lived through.

This struggle was most clearly illustrated, for the prisoners, by their legal records, which flattened their complicated, unique experiences into generic, one-dimensional convictions: first-degree murder, assault with a deadly weapon, manslaughter, destruction of property. This frustration with "everyday words" reminded me of a line in Conrad's *Lord Jim*, another novel narrated by Marlow, who complains that Jim's story is impossible to explain in a court of law, yet "they wanted facts. Facts! They demanded facts from him, as if facts could explain anything!"

Not all the prisoners agreed that *On the Yard* was realistic. Charles picked up on what he saw as inaccuracies in Braly's descriptions of prison life and found them difficult to let go. While he knew the book was a novel and not a memoir, he seemed to feel disappointed—perhaps even cheated—to find out that a published author was unable (as he saw it) to get the details right. Personally, I saw Braly's descriptions of prison architecture as a way of suggesting that human beings are inseparable from their context, and that the longer we live in a place, the more it becomes a part of our mind-set and physical makeup. But Charles had done time in San Quentin himself, although he was there after Braly, and he wasn't able to look at the descriptions objectively. He complained that the author had got a lot of things wrong. He'd got the chow hall wrong, and the tiers, and the way the cellblocks were structured, and even the yard. He went on pointing out the differences until the other men got annoyed.

"This is a work of fiction, Charlie," Kevin had to remind him eventually. "Suck it up."

NOVEMBER 14, 2013

Halfway through our discussion the following week, a CO came to the door of the classroom and beckoned for me to step outside. A short, light-skinned African-American woman in a wavy wig, she was one of the officers who always made things difficult for me. I'd once overheard her complaining to a colleague that she hated working in the commissary because the prisoners would come close enough she could smell their breath. She'd called me out of the room to reprimand me for the way I was sitting.

"The way you sit in that chair, everybody can see right up your skirt," she informed me.

I'd been very conscious of the way I'd been sitting, and I wouldn't have been let inside if my skirt hadn't come down well over my knees. I assumed the CO wanted a reason to show her power, and this was the first that came to mind. I thanked her politely for her advice. I didn't want to cause any trouble.

By now the men were well into *On the Yard*. We were discussing Braly's descriptions of the prison's physical structure, and one scene in particular where we get to know the building's secret, nocturnal life. A character named Cool Breeze leads a friend, Banales, through the paint shop and into the boiler room, where secret card games take place at night. Cool Breeze is smiling with guilty excitement "like a child who has discovered a secret passage within the walls of his own home, and thus restored his faith in the marvelous and forbidden world just beyond the threshold of his own experience." He gives cigarettes to the attendant, who leads them to the central boiler and opens the door. Inside the empty boiler, lit by a single light bulb, seven men are sitting in a circle playing a secret crap game.

We also discussed the grotesque and fascinating Sanitary Slim (a shoe-shine fetishist). When Slim is around, especially at night, each character's emotional anxiety is palpable. He's definitely a creepy character, yet at the same time I couldn't help also sympathizing with Slim. What compelled me most of all was the psychological truth of these presentations, the hypnotic effect of each character's inner voice. However outlandish and one-dimensional characters like Sanitary Slim and Gasolino might seem at first, they're revealed to have deep, rich inner lives.

But Kevin wasn't convinced.

"Another book that turned queer," he complained.

He was referring to the fact that prison tough guy Chilly Willy meets his downfall when an astute and manipulative prison psychiatrist installs him in a cell with a piece of "stuff" by the name of Candy Cane. Chilly Willy, who's less sexually so-phisticated (and less heterosexual) than he seems, quickly sub-mits to the allure of his seductive new cellmate.

"I just don't want to read about that shit," Kevin continued, closing his copy of *On the Yard* and laying it down on his tray table. "I tell you what: that guy—or that bitch, I should say—wouldn't last long in this prison."

This fired everyone up, and they started to talk about how the fictional characters in *On the Yard* could be compared to well-known personalities at JCI. As I listened to the men talk, I no-ticed how, in their conversation, the planes of novel and reality seemed to overlap. The prisoners all knew plenty of men con-demned as "baby rapers," like the novel's Will Manning, a gentle soul convicted of having sex with his teenage stepdaughter (he did it, though his wife set him up). They also nominated candi-dates for JCI's versions of prison kingpin Chilly Willy and of Sheldon "Stick" Wilson, the sociopathic leader of a three-person gang of neo-Nazi thugs.

"I was pissed about Charlie Wong," declared Turk. "He was the best. Turned out he was a snitch!"

Everyone liked Turk. He had an easy way of talking that was difficult to resist. His black prison-issue glasses rested on slightly

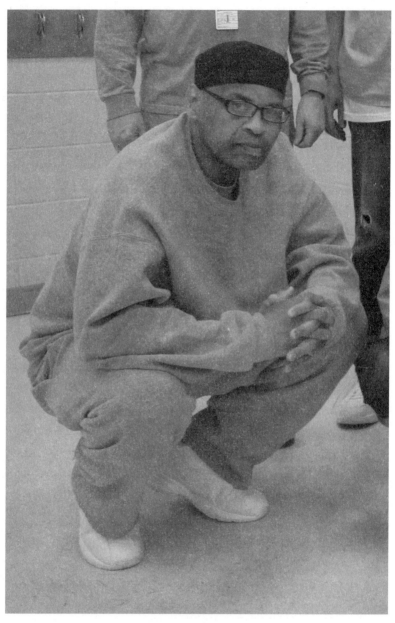

TURK

pointed ears, a gold tooth gleamed when he smiled, and he always wore a black skullcap. Since, like Donald, he worked at the woodshop, he usually wore Timberland work boots, gray sweatpants, and a gray sweatshirt. At first he wouldn't tell me how old he was ("I only tell the doctor and police my age"); later, I found out he was sixty-three and already a great-grandfather. He'd been married "several times" and had recently remarried his first wife, Sharon. He had five biological children (two of them named David) and a number of stepchildren. A sixth biological child, Dante, had been killed in 2001. To honor his son, Turk had had his back tattooed with a text that, since he had no access to a full-length mirror, he couldn't recall. "I think the words go something like this," he told me. " 'I remain loyal to the code of silence, true to our brotherly love. If I ever betray the bond of friendship, slander my character, slay me, eradicate my existence, death before dishonor.' That's not exactly it, but it's close. Sometime I'll let you see it for yourself."

Although he was always the first to fall asleep when the room got hot (which was pretty often), Turk was, for the most part, a lively presence. When it was his turn to read, he'd do so slowly and dramatically, pointing at the words on the page, stopping occasionally to comment ("I like that!"). His written responses were always unpredictable. Like a lot of the men, he used a typewriter most of the time; when he wrote by hand, he produced a semi-legible, right-slanted scrawl that mixed capital and lowercase letters, sometimes fitting only four or five words on each line. He would often begin his written papers with a greeting ("Good morning. How are you?"), and his responses were peppered with questions (both actual and rhetorical), exclamation points, and addresses to the reader. He always signed them "Turk F. Bey," followed by the date.

Although he was always good-natured and playful in the book club, Turk, I learned, had caused more than his share of trouble. He grew up, he told me, "on the unforgiving streets of Baltimore City and in the Maryland Penitentiary," and first arrived at JCI in October 1991, when he was forty: he had received a life sentence for "murdering a drug dealer who refused to stay away from my fifteen-year-old son." In 1993 he was sent to the supermax in Cumberland for three years as a result of infractions. In 1997, while being transported from the prison, he tried to escape, shooting a guard in the process. He was quickly recaptured and convicted of first-degree assault, carrying a concealed deadly weapon with intent to injure, and reckless endangerment. In March 2002 he was transferred a to prison in New Mexico, where he remained until 2011, when he was brought back to JCI.

Now he was involved with JCI's Friend of a Friend program, a group that mentors young prisoners and teaches them how to interact with people in prison, how to deal with their families and keep them close, and how to talk to their caseworkers and to the COs without being confrontational. He told me that, other than Friend of a Friend, the book club was the only program he'd been involved in since entering prison more than twenty-eight years ago that had "worked" for him. "Say we didn't have this group. We'd be on lockup down the road somewhere," he said of himself and his pal Donald. "This is the longest either of us has been on general population in a whole lot of years."

Turk's head, it turned out, was a sign of his membership in the Moorish Science Temple of America, one of the prison's twenty religious groups, nine of which were Muslim. These included well-established denominations such as Sunnis, as well as groups like the Nation of Islam, the Lost-Found Nation of Islam, and the Nation of Gods and Earths. Seventy-five percent of the prisoners at JCI were African-American, and most of them were members of one or another of these sects.

The prison's many religious groups were widely believed by prison authorities to be "jailhouse religions," meaning beliefs that would disappear as soon as the follower was released from prison. I'm not sure what the difference is between "jailhouse" religions and "real" religions; after all, many people take up religious beliefs in a time of crisis and let them go when things improve. At JCI, however, the boundaries between the various sects seemed more fluid and less decisive than those of "outside" religious groups, despite the fact that the different sects at JCI were often at odds. The real concern with the enthusiastic espousal of religion in the prison, I suspect, was that it bonded some men too closely—in a gang-like way, perhaps—with their fellow congregants, and it isolated others so greatly in the private study of their religious texts that they were too much alone.

NOVEMBER 21, 2013

The following week, the men continued discussing characters they liked and identified with in *On the Yard* until a comment from Sig silenced the room.

"We're all seeing parallels between these characters like Manning, Nunn, Stick, Sanitary Slim, and other guys here at JCI," he said, "but I haven't noticed anybody here recognizing himself."

The forty-four-year-old Sig was an imposing figure, with a shaved head, a short, neatly trimmed beard, and too-tight prison-issue glasses that, when he took them off, left horizontal indentations on the sides of his head. His arms were tattooed with guns and Confederate flags, and when he smiled you could see a gap from a missing tooth on the right side of his mouth. On his right

SIG

hand he wore a large, thick ring embossed with a pentagram; around his neck hung a Thor's hammer pendant; sometimes he wore a denim cap hand-embroidered with esoteric insignia (at JCI, sewing and embroidery were skills in high demand). On the cover of his exercise book he'd glued a photo of a nude blonde, her arms coyly covering her breasts.

"We all identify with Juleson," he went on. "But that may not be how other guys see us."

"So who do you identify with?" asked J.D. curiously.

"I don't like to admit it," replied Sig, "but I see a lot of myself in Society Red. I'm a repeat offender. I'm getting old. I'm probably going to spend the rest of my life inside."

Sig was smart and amiable. When I'd asked him about his family, he told me he'd been born and brought up in Essex, Maryland, the son of a truck driver, but his parents were now dead. "I had three half brothers from my mother's previous marriage, all older than me. One was sent to prison for cutting a guy's throat, and one got into drugs. They're both dead now. The one that's still alive I never really knew. He was eighteen when I was born and was sent to Vietnam when I was still a baby. We never even lived under the same roof."

Like most of the other prisoners, Sig had a long criminal record that described twenty years of violent crimes, including multiple counts of battery, assault with a deadly weapon, and lesser offenses like trespassing and the possession of drugs and firearms. In 1986, at sixteen, he was convicted of attempted murder and a handgun violation, and served ten years. "I learned to wear a mask in prison," he told me. "I started weight training to get physically stronger, and learned to make and carry a lot of different kinds of weapons, both actual and psychological."

He was currently serving a life sentence for a murder that

was "successful," as he put it. In August 1997, the twenty-eight-year-old Sig and a friend had killed a man by running over him with his own car. Sig's friend, who claims he was in the backseat at the time, turned state's evidence, pleading guilty to manslaughter in exchange for an eight-year sentence and an agreement to testify against Sig, who, he claimed, had tried to frame two men for the murder by trading them the victim's car in exchange for drugs. Sig was convicted in a death penalty trial and spent some time on death row before his sentence was commuted to life without parole.

Society Red, the character identified by Sig as his counterpart in *On the Yard*, is a nasty, clownish buffoon who's spent thirty of his forty-five years behind bars and has lost any ability to function in the world beyond the prison gates. The fact that Sig recognized himself in this unwholesome chump showed me that he had the capacity to see himself as others saw him. It also showed me that, like Paul Juleson, he'd been damned by himself as well as by the court.

Steven said he could see some of himself in Stick, the silent psychopath. I assumed he was just trying to jump on the bandwagon and impress Sig by identifying, like his friend, with an unlikable character.

I'd always thought of Steven as Sig's protégé. Once I'd asked Sig about it.

"In a way, you could say that," he'd replied, "but it's like pearls before swine. He's another victim of a broken system and he started out behind the eight ball, so only so much can be expected. He's a good kid, though."

Sig and Steven were two of the nine members of the Noble Hearth, the prison's Asatru clan. Asatru is a form of neopaganism; each Asatru member takes on a Nordic name. (Sig, for example, is short for Sigtrygg, "Victory Faithful.") In some federal prisons—although not in the wider community—Asatru is seen as a toned-down version of white nationalism; in fact, it's sometimes regarded as the "acceptable" public face of the Aryan Nation. When I asked Sig whether this was true, he said it wasn't—at least, not in JCI.

"I heard the Aryan Brotherhood started as an Irish gang; I think it was the Bluebirds," he told me. "The only connection between us and the Aryan Brotherhood is that they use some of our symbols. I think some of them also call themselves Odinists, but I don't know how many." Later, I found out there was a contingent of Aryan Nation adherents at JCI, but they were opposed to the Noble Hearth and kept trying to break it up and annex its followers.

The Noble Hearth was a loose affiliation, and for a long time its members weren't permitted to meet for ceremonies because the prison authorities saw it not as a religious group but as a gang, and they have a zero-tolerance policy for gang membership, especially after the BGF indictments. But Sig and his friends protested that Asatru wasn't a gang or a cult but a religion based on ancestors and the earth. They had no interest in race or nationalism, he said. He and his friends found it unfair that the other men were allowed to celebrate their faiths and learn about their histories and that their religious leaders were permitted to come into prison to lead ceremonies. Meetings of the Moorish Science Temple were led by a pair of grand sheiks, two short men in billowing white shirts and red fezzes I'd seen at the prison's annual volunteers' luncheon. Jewish prisoners received kosher meals and could attend Jewish services. Others, like Buddhists and Rastafarians, weren't given a public platform but adherents were allowed to practice alone, in their cells. After threatening to take JCI to court for refusing to grant them their First Amendment rights, the Noble Hearth finally got its own time in the chapel.

"We're interested in our ancestral religion," Sig said of the Noble Hearth. "We're proud of our beliefs and our heritage." He said they believe in keeping their minds and bodies clean and in good shape. They don't do drugs, they read to keep their brains sharp, and they work out to stay healthy.

In *On the Yard*, the psychopathic Stick, as a teenager, is obsessed with drawing swastikas on the walls around him. His schoolbooks are covered in them. "He wasn't the first boy to have found a kind of negative magic in this discredited symbol," writes Braly. "In a way its banality was almost reassuring." Another figure in *On the Yard* who creates a form of worship in his daily life is Solitary Slim, whose compulsive cleanliness has developed into a religious fervor. "He was equal death on dirt and disorder and he made no firm distinction between the two forms of contagion. Sparkling toilets and a rigid anus were equally wholesome." Slim is permitted to clean prisoners' footwear in the evenings, since few staff members realize that the "steaming drive" of his sexual release is obtained solely from shining shoes.

Although I recognized neither a Stick nor a Solitary Slim among the men I knew at JCI, outside of organized religious groups, the prisoners fell readily into what might be described as makeshift or syncretic belief systems, cults whose forms of worship sprang from any ingredients close at hand. Sig and Steven's Asatru symbols contained a similar kind of "negative magic" to Stick's swastikas, for example, as did prison tattoos, which seemed to be popular mainly with the younger men. From what I could tell, the white guys were either covered with them or had none at all. Older men sometimes had a few faded tattoos from the past but rarely seemed to get new ones. I'd heard that prison tattooists would discourage young prisoners from getting their first stick-and-poke tattoos, since they might come to regret signs of their identity as an ex-con. But once a guy's been in the system for a while and knows he might never stand a chance of parole, he'll start to acquire tattoos to confirm his identity as a convict.

Steven and Sig had very few places on their arms that weren't tattooed, and even though he had only a year or so left to serve, Steven seemed to be working to fill in the gaps. Most of their tattoos were monochrome, but sometimes they mixed ink with melted-down paint chips (no doubt full of lead) scraped from the walls of their cells. I got the impression that, for most of the men, tattooing was about marking them as belonging to the same culture as well as distinguishing group members from one another.

One day Steven rolled up his right shirtsleeve to show me a garish display of monstrous skulls and voluptuous ladies.

"This is the demonic woman," he said, pointing to a buxom red she-devil on his right inner forearm. "My friend did this lady here. She's lustful, she's not afraid to express herself sexually, and she's just beautiful." He then turned his arm over to display the word "Legion" written in a cursive font on his outer left forearm. "The same guy did this one as well. It's the name I've given myself to reflect the different aspects of my personality." Next he turned his arm over and showed me a Celtic cross on the back of his right wrist. "I did this one myself, in honor of my Welsh heritage."

At first I considered the Noble Hearth, with its runes and sigils, to be a kind of Nordic never-never land into which men like Sig and Steven could escape—a childish fantasy fueled by regressive yearnings. Later I realized how wrong I was. The prisoners' tribal signs and symbols fulfilled a serious adult need, and tattooing them on their flesh was a way of establishing or reaffirming community, either with those who were left outside—via names and messages like Turk's elegy to his dead son—or with those who are inside, or both. In many cases, the gang is the convict's first experience of order, whether on the street or in prison. These were men who'd never managed to fit into the social groups the rest of us belong to. Either they'd never been married or they'd been married too many times. A few, like Charles, were married to someone they'd met while in prison. Some, like Vincent and J.D., had no children at all; others, like Steven and Sig, had children they'd never seen or hadn't seen for many years; the rest had spreading clans of children, stepchildren, and grandchildren, often by different women. None of them went to church regularly before coming to prison. Kevin and Donald had both belonged to the military briefly. In a sense, the prison's sects and gangs provided them with more community and support than they'd ever had on the outside, and gave them a permanent, stable family, which would always be in place no matter what.

DECEMBER 5, 2013

In our final meeting to discuss *On the Yard*, we were joined for the last time by Guy, who was about to be released. Since coming out of lockup, he'd been sharing a cell with Charles. This pleased me, since Charles made sure Guy did the reading for the book club and that he took it seriously.

I hadn't seen Guy for more than six months, and he looked even more waiflike than ever in his ridiculously oversized jeans.

He was carrying all his possessions in a duffel bag: he was worried they'd call for him anytime. When I asked him what his plans were, he told me he wanted to go to college. I gave him my e-mail address and asked him to get in touch. I said I'd help him if I could. Most prisoners aren't released directly from JCI but taken to a pre-release facility for a week or so, to prepare them for life on the outside. Then, once they've met their parole officers and arranged the details of their parole, they're free to go.

Later, when Guy had left the prison, I asked the other prisoners whether they thought he'd manage to keep out of trouble. Those who knew him well had serious doubts.

"Guy's a drug addict," said Charles, flatly. "He needs to get himself a place in rehab. That's the only chance he's got."

"He can't function sober," added Donald, whose DPSCS sweatpants had been mended with a patch that said "No Fear." The neat stitching on the patch reminded me of Donald's perfect handwriting, its clear printed capital letters embellished with subtle, unexpected curls and flourishes. It also reminded me of the hot-air balloon sewn over many years by one of the convicts in *On the Yard* whose fabric is studied by accident investigators who find it to be weakened as a result of excessive stitching, "an analogy to hesitation marks in a suicide."

"If he's coming back, maybe we should save his place in the book club," I said, half seriously.

"I don't think he'll be back," said Donald. "Tell the truth, I think he's going to OD."

About a month after his release, on January 10, 2014, I got an e-mail from the account of a woman whose name I didn't recognize. It was Guy, using—I assumed—his aunt's e-mail address. "Hello," he wrote. "Just wanted to touch base with you and see how you are doin. Im doin OK. Is there anyway you could help me out with more information on college. Feel free to reply back to this email. Would like everyone to know I say Hello."

I replied the same day, sending him information about college financing. (Many ex-prisoners are eligible for grants, but not, unfortunately, those convicted of drug offenses, which Guy had been.) "Where are you living?" I wrote. "If you're anywhere near downtown Baltimore, I'll buy you a coffee." There was no reply.

6

MACBETH

I first read *Macbeth* when I was thirteen. The edition of the play we were given at school was neither a hardback nor a paperback but a hybrid of the two, with a bendable red cover, published by J. Dent and Co. in 1906. Like most things about my school, it had seen better days. In the margins of my copy, students before me had scrawled obscenities, blaming Shakespeare for their boredom.

The reigning educational theory of the time was the principle of "mixed ability," which meant no streaming or sorting. It was considered unfair to single out any student for their application or achievements. There was no honor roll, no grade point average; very few students at my school were expected to go to college, and even fewer wanted to. Most of the time, I was frustrated and depressed, but there were teachers who went out of their way to help me. My English teacher was among them—a good-natured, old-fashioned man who, when he realized how much I loved to read, gave me extra lessons to help prepare me for university entrance exams.

It's strange, looking back, to realize how little I knew about Mr. Johnson. I had no idea where he was from, where he had gone to college, whether he had a wife or family. I didn't even know his first name. At school he was known as an "anorak" or "boffin"—the British equivalent of "nerd" or "geek." He was shortsighted and absentminded, with unkempt eyebrows, rosacea, and oversized glasses that would keep slipping down his nose, and he had a nervous habit of sniffing every time he pushed them up. None of this put me off, although I was slightly dismayed when, on leaving school one day, I caught sight of him furtively smoking a cigarette at the bus stop, looking a little seedy. Never mind. I admired him for his intelligence and his love of literature, not his looks or his hygiene. I was honored that he'd singled me out for special treatment. He thought I deserved better.

I wish I'd been more appreciative of the time and attention Mr. Johnson offered me. Like most teenagers, I was graceless and awkward, caught up in my own affairs; I probably didn't even thank him. On the other hand, the school must have been even more frustrating for him than it was for me—after all, I was just passing through—and the time we spent reading Shakespeare may have been as rewarding for him as it was for me. I hope so.

When I read *Macbeth* for the first time, I understood almost nothing. The play's immediate subjects (kingship, Scottish history, nations at war) did not engage me, nor did I have any interest in theater. I loved *Macbeth* not for its story but for its language. I was fascinated by the weight of the words, their sequence and rhythm, the way they made me feel, even though they were often incomprehensible. Reading them, whether aloud or in my head, was like listening to a religious service in an archaic language. Not knowing what they meant made my faith even stronger, and their darkness had a profound effect on my imagination.

At school in the 1970s, all you got was the text itself. Nothing came between you and the book. When I handed out copies of *Macbeth* at JCI, it felt like things had come full circle. Due to the restrictions of the prison, there was nothing between the men and *Macbeth*. There was, however, a major difference between the prison class and my own first encounter with the book. I'd chosen an edition with a modern translation opposite the original on each page, and although we mostly read aloud from the translation, we often went back over the original, as I wanted the men to get a sense and feel for Shakespeare's language.

FEBRUARY 11, 2014

We reconvened after the holiday break on a chilly day in February. I'd had an awful winter. Grisby, my beloved French bulldog, died unexpectedly at the end of January while staying overnight at the vet's. He'd been in decent health and was only eight years old. There'd been changes among the men too. Guy had been released. Kevin had been having so many seizures he'd been transferred to a different prison, with better medical resources.

Vincent, whose release date was also rumored to be coming up, had chosen two new men to replace them. A tall middle-aged lifer with receding hair and a boyish grin took the place left by Guy. This was Nick, who'd been convicted of a high-profile murder as a young man. He was enthusiastic, respectful, and polite, and fit right in, mainly because he already knew Steven and Sig and was a member of the Noble Hearth. A wiry, surly young African-American guy with dreadlocks took Kevin's place. This was Day-Day.

Day-Day had been a student in my psychology class, and at the time, to be honest, I'd found him slightly scary. He had tattoos all over his body: flames climbed his legs; stars dotted his arms; his knuckles spelled out the words "God's Gift"; and an ornate letter *h* was etched between his eyes. He'd told me that he suffered from bipolar disorder, and he often seemed on the verge of a violent explosion. At the time, I asked him if he'd had an outlet for his anger.

"Yeah," he'd replied. "When I get stressed, I talk to my shrink. She put on this nice music and I just walk up and down and get out my rage."

He'd served a nine-year sentence, then a five-year sentence, and four and a half years of his current thirty-year sentence for "armed robbery, assault, handgun, drugs, PCP, cocaine, E-pills, weed." Day-Day was so skinny and young looking it was hard for me to believe he was over thirty. He addressed the other men in a low drawl, but with me he used a fast mumble; both were difficult for me to understand at first, especially since everything he said was laced with street talk and profanities. Yet, before long, I developed an ear for it.

Day-Day's written work was fascinating. He used sheets torn from someone else's notebook. His dotty scrawl slanted heavily to the right, with big spaces between the words and a thick margin. He used virtually no punctuation apart from the occasional smiley face, and his thoughts were unfettered by grammar and unfiltered by any internal censor. At first I was surprised Vincent had chosen him for the book club, but before long he became one of the most committed members of the group, and his responses to the books, though idiosyncratic, showed a sympathetic engagement that took me by surprise.

Most of the men were wearing heavyweight, long-sleeved thermals under their DPSCS blues. I asked them what had been going on since I'd last seen them. It was a tactless and insensitive question—nothing much happens in prison, and when it does, it's almost always bad news.

"My sister passed away," someone offered. "She was seventy-six. I just heard the news last night."

"I'm sorry to hear that," I said. "Was she your only sister?"

"No, I've got five."

"In that case, I guess you can spare one." I immediately cursed myself. It was a stupid joke, and not at all funny. No one even smiled. To atone for my gaffe, I told them about Grisby's death. As I was speaking, I realized some people might think it insensitive of me to equate the two. I trailed off, feeling ridiculous.

"Anyone else have any news?" I tried again.

There was a long pause.

"I've been in the hospital," said Charles. "I've been having problems with my eyes."

For the first time, I noticed he looked drained. He was wearing dark glasses, and I could see the strain of a recent ordeal in his face.

"What happened?" I asked.

Charles gave a rusty chuckle. "It sounds kind of funny. I was having a bad dream, and I poked myself in the eye. It probably wouldn't have done any serious damage, only I've had this cataract for the last two years. I've tried to get to see the eye doctor to get it removed, but they really don't care. They said to me, 'As long as you've got one eye that works, that's all you need.' Anyway, because of the cataract, when I injured myself, the retina and the iris got damaged, and they had to take me out to University of Maryland hospital for an emergency operation."

"At least you got out of prison for a while," I said. "That must have been a nice change."

"No it wasn't. They had me handcuffed to the hospital bed by an arm and a leg. After the operation, I had to wear this plastic shield over my head until the damage had healed. I couldn't lie down or shift position because of the handcuffs. I was in so much pain I couldn't sleep."

"Didn't they give you any medication?"

"They gave me something every six hours, but it wore off after four. Then they stopped giving me anything. They said it ran out. Said it was on back order. They'd put a catheter into my bladder because of the handcuffs—I couldn't get up to go to take a piss—and it gave me a bladder infection. Felt like I needed to piss all day long."

"That sounds awful. How are you doing now?"

"I'm feeling a little better every day." He showed me his damaged eye underneath his glasses; it was bloodshot and badly swollen. "I need to keep it covered up to protect it. They said it's going to take about two months for the eye to heal enough for them to do the follow-up surgery and insert the new lens. And that's only if the surgery's approved by the medical department."

The other men were listening to Charles with sympathy, but without surprise. They'd all had similar experiences, or knew someone who had. Naïvely, I'd assumed that a trip out of the prison, even if it was to the hospital, must have been a pleasant change from the monotonous daily routine. Later, I came to realize how wrong I was. Trips "uptown," whether to the hospital or the courtroom, meant the prisoner had to change into the requisite orange jumpsuit and "three-piece jewelry" (leg irons, waist chains, and handcuffs) and then sit in a hallway, often for hours at a time, waiting for paperwork to be filled out. If the paperwork wasn't ready in time or if anything was missing, the appointment would be rescheduled, and another day would be spent the same way.

It's difficult to walk in leg irons, so the CO accompanying the prisoner is supposed to hold his arm or waist chain to keep him from falling if he loses his balance. One of the men told me that once, when he was coming back from court, the CO who was supposed to be guiding him literally dropped him on his face, causing him to break his nose and lose most of his teeth. Later, when reading *Macbeth*, I wondered if the men found the play's violence so engaging because, compared to the pointless, undignified brutality of prison life, it's always important and purposeful, which may be why Shakespeare lingers on it so deliberately. We agreed that these descriptions of bloodshed provided some of the best lines in the play.

I asked the men whether any of them had heard of *Macbeth*. Most of them recognized the title but knew nothing about it, not even that it was a play by Shakespeare, which surprised me, since literature is usually more a part of school experience than art or music. But then, I recalled, many of these men hadn't had much schooling, or hadn't paid much attention if they had.

"I'd always assumed Macbeth was a girl," said Charles.

"I never heard of *Macbeth*, but I heard of this cat Shakespeare," said Turk.

I told them the play was written sometime between 1604 and 1606, when England and Scotland had just been united under the Scottish king James. I said some people thought Shakespeare wrote the play specifically to please the king, who was interested in witches and demons. I also told them about the superstition surrounding the play. I said some people thought if you pro-nounced the title in the theater, you'd be cursed.

"Like Bloody Mary," said Day-Day.

"Right," I said. "So who wants to read?"

At first, it was a little crazy. The men were confused by the layout of the lines on the page. Every so often, one of them would start reading the original lines on the facing page rather than the translation. Another would read the stage directions as part of the text, and someone else would forget who they were sup-posed to be. Everyone struggled with the names, especially Gla-mis and Cawdor. Still, we managed to wrestle our way through the first few scenes before the CO came in to take the count.

"So what did you make of your first day of Shakespeare?" I asked them when the CO had left.

"I love it," said Steven. Others weren't so easily satisfied. Charles said he was having trouble reading aloud and under-standing what was happening at the same time. "I'm going to have to read it again back in my cell," he said. His damaged eye can't have helped. Donald said he guessed he could get used to it. Sig, who had on a black knitted cap with a silver snowflake de-sign, said he liked the history—the Scottish lords, their wars, and the violence.

"And the witches," added Steven. "Gotta love those witches."

"Do you think they're lying?" I asked him.

"Sure," said Steven. "Witches are always bad, right? That's what makes them witches."

"Uh-uh," disagreed Donald. "What about Glinda the Good Witch?"

"Yeah," Turk joined in. "What about that chick Samantha in *Bewitched?*"

"What about Jeannie in *I Dream of Jeannie?*" added Vincent. "I dreamed about her a lot, I can tell you."

"Why do you think they chose Macbeth?" I asked.

"They know he's ambitious," suggested Sig. "They probably know he secretly wants to be king."

"Or maybe they know he's susceptible," I said. "It's possible they know he'll twist what they say to match what he wants to believe. Look at Banquo's lines in Act I, Scene III, where he warns Macbeth about the witches' prophecies. 'Oftentimes, to win us to our harm, / The instruments of darkness tell us truths, / Win us with honest trifles, to betray's / In deepest consequence.'"

"That's an old courtroom trick," said Donald. "They say something that you agree with and you start nodding, then they add a lie to the end of it, and before you realize it you're agreeing to some bullshit they've loaded on you."

"I think you've got it," I said, impressed.

As I drove home that day, I figured most of the men hadn't really been able to follow much of the text, but I wasn't worried. When I'd first read the play myself, I remember being fascinated by the images conjured up by the strange words on the page. I had the feeling I was somehow reading through the language to the direct emotion beneath. In a way, my lack of understanding served to fire my half-formed imagination, making the words even more evocative than they rightly should have been. For example, in Act III, Scene IV, Macbeth refers to "maggot-pies." When I first read this phrase, I pictured a worm-encrusted pastry in an old-fashioned chafing dish, with a gravy boat full of blood on the side. Now I know that "maggot-pie" is an archaic term for a magpie; the "correct" meaning, when I learned it, was disappointing compared to the one I'd made up in my head.

For this reason, I like to stay open to misreadings. My own misapprehensions often give me what I need at the time. They become a tool, a way for me to get somewhere I need to go. Unconsciously, perhaps, I often misread for my own purposes. When I first read *Macbeth*, it was my ignorance that stirred my dormant consciousness, like a spell being cast. I was hoping some of the same magic that worked on me might also work on the men.

FEBRUARY 18, 2014

When I arrived at the prison for our second session on *Macbeth*, the sky was clear, banks of dirty snow were piled up against the fence, and four seagulls were perched on the roof of the administration building. Outside the schoolroom door, Charles was waiting for me, slouched against the wall like a wayward teenager. He complained that the CO on duty wouldn't let him in until it was time for our group to start, which the CO claimed was 2:15. Charles said it was supposed to begin at 2:00. I thought so, too, but, afraid to contradict the officer, I asked if he'd mind letting Charles in early so we could "go over his homework."

In the classroom, Charles told me his eyes were still bothering him. He was supposed to have another operation but it had been difficult for him to get an appointment with the eye doctor, and all the waiting around had been taking its toll. He was able to read today, however, so I asked him if he'd mind reading the part of Macbeth. I wanted a good reader for the buildup to the murder scene, and I knew Charles wouldn't let me down. I asked Turk, with his sonorous voice, if he'd mind reading the part of Lady Macbeth, whom we'd yet to meet. I liked to watch Turk read as much as I liked to listen to him. He'd run his finger along the lines, repeating things he didn't grasp completely, affirming sentiments he liked with the occasional "Mm-hmmm!" His energy more than made up for his errors in pronunciation.

"So what do you make of Lady Macbeth?" I asked, when we came to the end of the scene.

Day-Day's eyes lit up. "She strong," he said. "She know her man."

"Why does she keep making pokes at his manhood?" asked Charles.

"She hard," explained Day-Day. "She know him. She know he just a child. She, like, 'Are you gonna have a crown and be a coward? I rather kill my own child than go back on my word,' you feel me? You can tell she killed before, and he know it. He seen it."

"But he's killed too," I pointed out. "He's just been honored for it."

"He killed, but he only killed in war," argued Day-Day.

When we came to the murder scene, I was surprised how engrossed the men were. Each of them followed closely, many running their fingers along the lines like Turk, some of them mouthing the words silently as the readers spoke their parts. The room was unusually quiet and tense as the scene unfolded, the silence outside disturbed only by the occasional raised voices and laughter coming from the classroom next door, where a group was studying *The Purpose Driven Life: What on Earth Am I Here For?* by Rick Warren. During the murder scene itself, the men were alarmed by Macbeth's jittery behavior and annoyed with him for forgetting to leave the bloody daggers in Duncan's chamber with the grooms. As I listened to them, I realized that although I'd read *Macbeth* many times in many places with lots of different kinds of students, I'd never read it with people who knew what it felt like to commit murder.

After we'd finished reading, Day-Day looked up, his eyes gleaming. "See, when you got a man like that," he said, "he need a woman to take charge. She need to take control. She know he too scared to get what he want. She know he don't do nothing but talk."

"So she gives him the courage to kill the king," I said, "but he regrets it the very moment he's done it."

"Because now he lost," said Day-Day. "She make him kill outside of war. She make him step off his path. Before, he follow his king, he knew his path, you feel me? You step off your path, you lost."

"You wouldn't have done the same thing?" Turk asked him.

"I'd have killed the king, for sure, but I wouldn't have been no coward about it," said Day-Day. "I wouldn't have let her call me no child."

Day-Day seemed to understand Macbeth's mind better than anyone else. In fact, the more time I spent in his company, the more fascinating I found this young man, with his hard, skinny limbs and dirty mouth. I'd never met anyone like him. He was a curious mixture of loose (the lazy way he slouched in his seat, the big holes in his pants, the way he seemed to speak almost without moving his mouth) and tightly wound, although I no longer had the feeling he was a bomb about to go off. That day he had an orange elastic band wrapped around his wrist (orange, I later learned, was his gang color). He'd taken it out of his dreadlocks, which he was constantly twisting and stroking. I could sense the addictive pleasure it gave him.

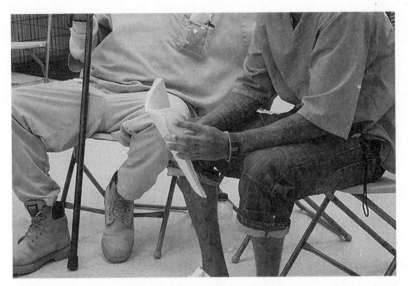

DONALD AND DAY-DAY

Day-Day seemed to have a visceral sense of just how pissed off Macbeth was about Malcolm being named prince of Cumberland. Yet he also believed that, if it hadn't been for his wife, Macbeth would have gone on feeling frustrated and rejected. He wouldn't have attempted to alter the course of fate. After the murder, Day-Day was convinced that, under his wife's pressure, Macbeth was going to crack and turn her in.

"He gonna turn state's evidence," he predicted.

MARCH 4, 2014

Sig was missing.

"He won't be coming today," said Donald. "He may not be here for a while."

"Why not?" I asked.

"He's on lockup."

"What for?"

"It's one of these nonsense charges."

"Was he in a fight?" I asked. Mostly, when men got sent to the lockup, it was either for a dirty urine test or for getting in a fight. Sig told me he didn't do drugs and I believed him, so I thought he must have been in a fight.

"Nope," sighed Donald. "You know how fucked-up things are around here, Mikita. Well, there was this new female CO taking the count on the tier, and she didn't really know how things are supposed to work. See, any female officer is supposed to announce that she's coming when she takes the count, so you got some privacy. Well, this new CO, she didn't know the rules. She caught Sig in a private moment and wrote him up on a charge."

"But if she didn't announce herself, wasn't it her fault?"

"You'd think so. You'd think she'd learn pretty quick, but no. She wrote up a whole lot of other guys for the same thing."

Later, when Turk arrived, Donald gave his friend some uncensored commentary on the same incident.

"Which one was it?" asked Turk. "The new one? Short girl? Kind of heavyset? Light-skinned?"

"No, no, no," said Donald. "You're thinking of a different girl. This is a different new one. She's short, real dark, and fat."

"They should have charged *her* with being a Peeping Tom," protested Turk. "Put *her* in the lockup!"

"You know what I do when they come to take the count?" said Donald. "I always do the same thing. The officer always gets to the tier at the same time, right? I always make sure I'm taking a shit, sitting right there on the pot, naked. If he's late, I just sit there with the newspaper. You don't want to give us our privacy, fine. I say, here I am. Right here. Take a good, long look."

By now I'd learned the difference between lockup, lockdown, and solitary confinement. During a lockdown, the whole prison—or part of it—comes to a standstill, and the men aren't allowed to leave their cells. Solitary confinement cells are used for men placed on protective custody (by their own request or by that of the administration), men on suicide watch, and men who've demonstrated violent behavior. Lockup, known officially as segregation, is the prison's most commonly used form of punishment. Cells in the lockup fit two men, but most of the time, if you're on lockup, you're on your own, and this can have devastating consequences. You might think there'd be some relief in getting private time for a change, but the truth is sudden isolation can be traumatic for men accustomed to constant human company and a predictable routine.

Yet Sig, when he returned to class, seemed stoical about the matter. He'd spent three weeks in segregation before finally getting a hearing, at which he claimed he'd been fast asleep when the offense was supposed to have occurred. According to the documentation, the CO claimed that, when she looked through the window of Sig's cell to take the count, "he rubbed his penis at me." Questioned further, she admitted his penis was "not fully exposed." The hearing officer concluded that whatever Sig had done or hadn't done, it hadn't been a deliberate act of indecent exposure. The fact that Sig was found not guilty seemed redundant, however, since he'd already spent three weeks on lockup. Apparently, situations like this aren't unusual. Men who are found innocent of infractions they're currently being punished for are simply switched from disciplinary to administrative segregation; the authorities assume they're probably guilty of some misdemeanor or other. They're in prison, after all.

Despite Sig's absence, the men were in a playful mood. When

I allocated roles, Steven begged to be the drunken porter, which was fine by me. I asked Nick if he'd mind reading the part of Lady Macbeth.

"Sure. I'm secure in my masculinity," he said, and proceeded to read the queen as a nagging wife with a high-pitched voice.

Turk, reading Macbeth, turned into a ham. "Please don't step on my lines, sir," he said to Day-Day, who'd started reading Turk's part by mistake.

"My bad, my bad," said Day-Day.

We were reading about the discovery of the murder, and the sounds of the prison made an appropriate backdrop. No sooner had Macduff declared, "Walk like ghosts to face this horror! Ring the bell" than a real bell rang in the hallway outside, making us almost jump out of our skin. When we came to the more difficult scenes, however, the men grew quiet and paid close attention to the text. At one point I glanced up from the book to see the CO looking in the classroom window from the hallway, gazing at us suspiciously, as if we were the ones who'd been plotting a murder.

We read from the discovery of Duncan's dead body to the scene in which Ross informs Macduff that his wife and family have been "savagely slaughtered" by Macbeth's executioners. Donald was reading the part of Ross, and after all the horror he returned to the playful mood that had reigned earlier in the afternoon.

"My children, too?" asks Macduff.

Donald couldn't help laying it on extra thick. "Wife, children, servants, dogs, cats, goats, you name it," Donald ad-libbed, turning one of the play's darkest moments into a joke. We all laughed with relief.

APRIL 1, 2014

I promised the men I'd bring in a film adaptation when we got to the end of *Macbeth*, and when the time came, I brought a copy of Roman Polanski's 1971 version, which is highly rated today, although at the time it was considered tastelessly brutal. For this reason if no other, I thought the men would enjoy it, although screening conditions were far from ideal. We had the TV with a twenty-inch screen again; we had to keep the lights on and the door open; and for the first time in many weeks, there was a lot of noise in the hall. Still, the men arrived prepared for a treat. J.D. brought his new training dog, Falcon. Steven had a new haircut, shaved on one side and flattened down at the front. There was candy from the commissary to share. Turk had brought mints and butterscotch; Charles brought a pack of Twizzlers. Nick had brought jelly beans to pass around. Like all other U.S. prisons today, JCI is smoke-free, and to some degree candy has replaced cigarettes as a sanctioned, legitimate treat. (I was told that contraband cigarettes were still sold; each one was cut into four or five hand-rolled smokes that went for two dollars apiece.)

The Polanski movie is my favorite Shakespeare adaptation, although I hadn't seen it for years and was worried it might not hold up. As it turned out, I found it as engaging as I'd remembered it and was soon deeply engrossed, despite the fact that the dialogue was hard to decipher in the noisy room and I really had to focus to hear properly. Over an hour had passed before I first became aware of the noises behind me. When I turned around, the first man I saw was Turk, slumped in his chair with his head on his chest. He was snoring rhythmically. Then I saw Day-Day, also asleep, his head down on his tray table. Steven, Sig, and Nick were all slumped down in their seats, snoozing. Vincent was yawning. J.D. and his dog had both nodded off. From what I could see, Charles and Donald were the only men still focused on the screen. I tried to get absorbed in the movie again, but now that I was aware of them, I couldn't block out the snores and yawns.

At the end of Act III, I stood up and paused the movie. The men stretched and roused themselves.

"What's up?" I asked.

"It's so boring," said Steven, standing up and stretching.

"We all know what's going to happen," said Sig with a huge yawn.

"What you don't understand, Mikita," explained Vincent, "is that these guys are used to watching fast action movies. They're all spoiled. They're not used to watching movies this old."

"Old? It's not old!"

"It's old," said J.D.

"Fine," I said. "You don't have to watch the rest of it. We can stop it here. Even though in the next scene Lady Macbeth sleep-walks in the nude."

This was enough to keep most of them awake for a while, and we made it through the rest of the movie.

Before I left that day, I had some news. Next session, I told them, a reporter from the *Baltimore City Paper* would be coming to the class with me. He was planning to write an article about the prison college program and about the reading group in particular. Vincent thought it would be a good idea if we planned an exercise to do in class, so I chose one from our textbook, which listed a number of projects in the back. The men would put themselves in the place of Macduff as he goes off to fight, and write a letter to Lady Macduff explaining why he felt the need to do so.

APRIL 15, 2014

I arrived at the prison with the *Baltimore City Paper* reporter, Baynard Woods; the photographer, J.M. Giordano; and Gerard Shields, the media relations officer from the Maryland Department of Public Safety and Correctional Services, whose job was to ascertain which men Woods could interview and—I imagine—to ensure nothing inappropriate was said. A tall man in worn white tennis shoes that clashed with his suit, Shields was a former reporter for the *New York Post* who'd only been with the DPSCS for three months. He'd covered Baltimore ex-mayor Martin O'Malley's first campaign for the *Baltimore Sun*, he told us, and after getting laid off from the *Post* he'd called in a favor from O'Malley's administration. He seemed a little uneasy in his new role.

Day-Day, who Woods describes in his article as "the young guy with the tattooed face," was the first to read his letter from Macduff.

"Hi, Babe," it began. "I miss you so much . . . You got me strung out. Whole time I'm out here, I'm thinking about that pretty body and that good pussy . . ."

I felt myself cringing and noticed some of the other men looking uncomfortable too. Shields was grimacing. Still, I know Day-Day was just completing the assignment as well as he knew how. Later, Donald told me he'd been trying to "groom" Day-Day in regard to how he should conduct himself in polite company. "He's got a big heart," said Donald. "He's just not there yet."

Eager to put the "good pussy" behind us, I asked Day-Day why, if Macduff misses his wife so much, he goes off and leaves her behind.

"Some things you gotta do," he said. "You know, being a gang member, for me, I would leave everybody for my gang. I could get married tomorrow, but if they call me, I got to go."

Gang membership, like "good pussy," was also taboo. I moved hastily on to the other men, who were, as Charles put it later, "playing their A game." Donald's letter was fabulous. "My sudden departure wasn't relative to you or family matters," he wrote. "You were made aware of the fact that, if you married me, you'd have to share my loyalties with king and country. I'm truly saddened because of our separation because duty calls."

There was a general murmur of approval. Everyone was impressed.

"Personally," said Donald, "I've written a thousand letters of that nature. I had a lot of explaining to do, just like Macduff."

"Did you ever leave voluntarily?" I asked him.

"Hell no."

I asked the men at what point they lost sympathy for Macbeth, if they did so at all.

"I was with him the whole time," said Day-Day. "Sometimes, when you fucked up, it's fucked."

"But he stays with it," I added.

"He stays with it," Day-Day agreed. "He take it the whole way through, fuck it. Even when they kill him at the end, his name still gonna ring."

The way he said it, you could tell that, in the future, Day-Day wanted his own name to ring.

Sig and Steven both said they had sympathy with Macbeth until he started taking things into his own hands. The moment Charles lost sympathy was when MacBeth started to lose his mind. Vincent lost sympathy when he realized Macbeth wasn't ready to be king.

"The man had no code," said Sig. "I have no respect for a man without a code."

"I respect him," said Turk, "but I have some reservations about the things that he did."

I felt proud of the men. They'd been eager to demonstrate to Woods the kind of thing we talked about each week in the reading group, including complex questions about law and loyalty. And they'd succeeded. In the car on the way home, Woods told me how much he'd enjoyed the discussion and how surprised he was by the men's enthusiasm and dedication.

"Would you say that was a typical meeting of the group?" he asked. His tape recorder was still running.

"Pretty much," I said. Then I remembered that we'd prepared an exercise, which wasn't something we'd ever done before. And the men hadn't had the chance to chat among themselves before class. That was usually when I got to hear them let off steam about everything going on in the prison.

"Though I guess I'd say they were on their best behavior," I added. "Most of the time, there's a lot more talk about . . ." I hesitated, unsure how to phrase it. "You know the guy with all the tattoos?" I asked.

Woods nodded.

"Well, more of his kind of talk," I said. I was struggling to come up with a shorthand description of Day-Day's style. "More talk about, you know, 'pussy.'"

Looking back, I want to tear my hair out.

7

STRANGE CASE OF

DR. JEKYLL AND MR. HYDE

When I picked up this short novella looking for books the prisoners might enjoy, it seemed very different from the familiar tale of the upright Victorian gentleman and his evil doppelgänger that I thought I knew. Rereading it, I realized *Jekyll and Hyde* is actually a detective story, and its major character is neither Jekyll nor Hyde but the man who solves the mystery: Jekyll's lawyer, a cordial fellow named Mr. Utterson. Jekyll appears only intermittently, and never speaks for himself until his written confession at the end of the book. Since *Jekyll and Hyde* is so short (it's less than a hundred pages and can be read in a single sitting), it seemed odd that I hadn't really engaged with it before. I must have been reading carelessly, breezing by on the assumptions I'd picked up from the movies.

Also, I'd assumed it was set in Edinburgh, where Robert Lewis Stevenson was born and raised, rather than in London (admittedly, the city is rarely named in the book). The London of *Jekyll and Hyde* is ugly, but it's a secret, sinister kind of ugliness: the dirt of the city is shrouded by fog and lamplight. Much of the action takes place under "a pale moon" or during damp winter mornings or evenings, when "the fog still slept on the wing above the drowned city" and "the lamps glimmered like carbuncles."

APRIL 22, 2014

I handed out copies of *Strange Case of Dr. Jekyll and Mr. Hyde* to the men (another no-frills version costing just a dollar) and, taking it for granted they'd be familiar with at least the title, asked them for their impressions of the story from movies they'd seen or from popular culture. Most of them knew its outline from *The Nutty Professor* (the 1996 remake with Eddie Murphy), although I was surprised that Day-Day had heard of neither the book nor of the phrase "Jekyll and Hyde."

The others were familiar with at least the split personality motif, and started talking about how their own personalities had changed when they were drunk or high.

"I used to get really friendly and give away all my stuff," said Nick.

"I'd usually get into fights," admitted Sig.

"I'd go the opposite way," laughed Steven. "I'd get real affectionate."

"Anyone ever turn into a completely different person?" I asked.

"I did," said Turk. "But that was because I was on the run."

"Same here," said Nick, with his big goofy grin. "I was twenty-one and I'd just received a twenty-five-year sentence for murder. I stole a car and bought a U.S. Army uniform from a thrift store.

I thought it would make people trust me. One night, I got pulled over by a cop after running a red light. I rolled down the window so he could see the stripes on my uniform. I said to him, 'I'm real sorry about that officer, but I'm trying to get back to the base before curfew. If you write me up for a citation, I'll be too late.' "

All the other men, I noticed, were listening closely. Even J.D.'s service dog, Falcon, had pricked up his ears.

"It worked. I couldn't believe it," continued Nick. "The cop goes, 'All right, Sergeant, go ahead.' I was in shock. You know, if he'd asked me anything—where was the base, what time was the curfew—I wouldn't have known what to say. But he just let me go. I thought, 'I can't wait to tell my buddies about this.' Then I remembered I was on the run. There was nobody to tell."

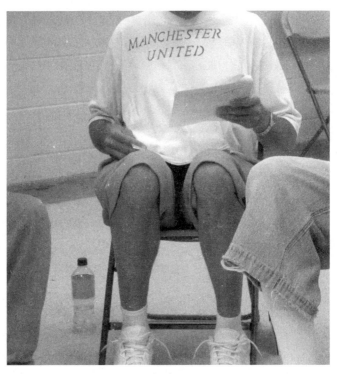

NICK

It was a good story, but I never knew how much of what Nick said was true. Sometimes I wondered if he even knew himself. He told me many times that he was from Cambridgeshire, but he didn't sound English and didn't seem familiar with British geography. He'd also told me that his older brother was over seven feet tall (this part I believed: Nick himself was six foot seven) and had recently died of shame because people kept making fun of his height. Nick told me he was serving a life sentence for the accidental death of his best friend, Danny, after they'd both taken LSD. Nick said he ran straight into Danny, knocking him into a tree and killing him.

The newspaper and court records tell a different story. In their account, Danny, a seventeen-year-old high school senior, went missing on an April afternoon in 1982. Nick, then nineteen, was the last person to see him; in fact, Nick had driven to Atlantic City in Danny's car (perhaps this was the kernel of his on-the-run story). Later, during the police investigation, Nick admitted to a friend who was wearing a wire that he'd killed Danny. Some of Danny's belongings were found in Nick's possession, and the police were convinced Nick was responsible for the murder. However, despite his taped confession, Nick couldn't be convicted of murder without a body, so in June of that year he was jailed for robbery and auto theft. Eight years later, when Danny's body was discovered buried in the woods, Nick received a murder conviction and a death sentence. He spent two years on death row before an appeals court voided his death sentence after considering mitigating evidence about his abusive upbringing.

Like most of the older guys at JCI, Nick had a couple of missing teeth. At first I assumed the men's bad teeth were a result of their lifestyle: too many drugs and cigarettes, too much coffee.

But my assumption was unconsidered, and I was thoughtlessly connecting bad teeth with bad habits. The answer was sadder and more straightforward. These men had lived for years with virtually no dental care, and instead of having their cavities filled, like those of us on the outside, they'd had the rotten teeth pulled out. For many years this was all the prison dentist was contracted to do. These men couldn't even get their teeth cleaned. If a prisoner got punched in the mouth, or broke his teeth after tripping and falling while in leg irons, the damage wasn't repaired. Recently, dental cleanings had been reintroduced, but the waiting list was very long: appointments with the hygienist were currently backed up for two years.

Despite his missing teeth and thinning hair, I could see that in his youth Nick must have been a handsome guy. Even now, at fifty-something, I could still see the shadow of his younger self. For some reason he always struck me as particularly clean, perhaps because his socks and sneakers looked especially white against his tanned skin. He told me he'd had two years of college before his arrest. When I first met him I found him likable and intelligent. After he'd been in the book club for a while, however, he began to annoy me. I started to find him loud, pushy, and a bit of a blowhard. I didn't believe a lot of what he said, and it took a while for me to come to terms with his overbearing personality. Now I feel as though I understand him a little better than I did at first; I'm learning to admire his resilience and self-sufficiency.

I introduced the men to Robert Louis Stevenson; we talked a little about his life and the novel's context, and then we began reading from the first chapter. Everyone read a section except Donald, who'd forgotten his reading glasses, and Charles, who was still having eye trouble. Although some of the men found

Stevenson's style a little wordy, they all agreed it was much easier to read than Shakespeare. I asked them to finish the first half of the novella before next week's meeting.

I walked back toward the prison gate with Charles, who wanted to tell me about a recent experience he'd had.

"It actually has a Jekyll-and-Hyde-type twist," he told me.

"Oh? What happened?"

"When Guy left," he began, "I got a new cellmate, this black guy in his mid-thirties. He seemed decent, and even though I'd always prefer to be on my own, I felt OK about sharing a cell with him. Now, this guy has no money, no visitors, and no job except a sewing gig now and then that brings him in a few dollars he uses to get high. He's got no possessions except an old analog television set that doesn't work. I like the guy and I think he's OK, so I look out for him. I share my coffee and snacks from the commissary. After six or seven weeks, this guy gets word from the court that he's won his appeal. He'll be heading back to Baltimore for a new trial. His lawyer doesn't think the state's attorney will want to retry him and they'll probably either drop all charges or offer him a deal to plead guilty and receive time served. Either way, he's looking to get out."

We passed through two sets of doors and out into the compound.

"So last week I have an appointment with a glaucoma specialist," Charles went on. "They take me downtown in chains and leg irons, and it's another useless waste of time. I'm waiting around to see him the whole day, and when I finally get to see this guy, he takes one look at me and tells me I don't have glaucoma. So they bring me back here. I'm standing outside my cell, waiting for the door to open, and this guy across the hall calls out to me, 'Hey, your cell buddy checked into protective custody. The sergeant brought him down here and packed him up a couple hours ago. You better check your stuff.'

"My cell door opens and I go inside. I can tell immediately that some things are missing. I make a list. Later, I find out he owed around two hundred dollars for drugs and other stuff he bought on credit. The items he stole from me were small. Trimmers, a book light, a PlayStation memory card, a couple of PlayStation games. Those games aren't cheap. He probably sold them or gave them to people he owed money to."

I knew video games were popular among the prisoners, but I felt oddly disappointed to learn that Charles had a PlayStation. I didn't know anything about them, and I assumed they were time-wasting toys for kids. Charles is close to seventy and a practicing Buddhist who meditates every day. I imagined him perhaps reading and writing in his spare time, not playing Grand Theft Auto or Ape Escape. Later, I learned that PlayStations can be used for all kinds of things: to watch movies, to listen to music, and to play games like chess and bridge that keep the memory quick and the brain sharp. I also remember it was Charles who'd set me straight about the cliché of prisoners having nothing but time on their hands. In prison, he'd told me, there's a set time for everything: meals, commissary, showers, school, religious services, gym, yard time, free time. You can't delay your meal for a few minutes, take an early shower, or postpone a task like you can on the outside. Everything you do is subject to detailed regulation. If you work, you might spend most of the day at your job, and when you've finished, had your dinner, and waited in line for a shower, it might be 6:00 or 7:00 p.m. You could get a couple of hours in the evening for writing letters and reading, although by then, he said, most people are too tired to do anything but watch television.

"Will you get your things back?" I asked.

"That's the thing. He'd already sold them. See, this guy is smart. He knew the date of my eye appointment. He must have been planning this for a while. He'd already found buyers for my stuff, and they'd already paid him. On top of that, he'd been getting drugs on credit and he'd run up a huge debt. The guy I know across the tier told me I should write up an ARP."

"What's that?"

"Administrative remedy procedure. He said I should put him and his cell buddy down as witnesses. The sergeant was wrong for allowing this guy to check into protective custody and to pack his stuff while I wasn't there. The next day the sergeant admitted it was his fault and said if we can't get my stuff back, he'd take me to the confiscated property room and I could choose things of equal value."

By now we'd reached the fence outside E and F blocks, where we went in different directions.

"Do you think you'll find similar things in the property room?" I asked him.

"You know, I hate to say it," he said, "but I may make out even better this way."

"So what's the problem?"

"I'm just real pissed at myself for letting my guard down. After all I've been through, I think I'm pretty skilled at assessing men's characters. It really shook me up to find I'd miscalculated so badly. I thought this guy was Dr. Jekyll, but as soon as my back was turned, he changed into Mr. Hyde."

APRIL 29, 2014

More bad news: Donald wasn't in class. According to Turk, he'd been sent to Patuxent Institution, the nearby correctional mental health center, for a mandatory "risk assessment."

"How long will that take?" I asked in dismay. Over the last year or so, I'd come to rely on Donald. He was one of the smartest men in the group, and he'd never missed a single meeting. He'd told me more than once that the book club had been instrumental in keeping him out of trouble. I believed him.

"Could be anything from sixty days to six months, depending on how many men they're assessing," said Turk stoically.

"Assessing for what?"

"Parole. Any time they're thinking about giving a lifer a recommendation for parole, they want to see if you can pass the risk assessment. If you come out looking good, they send your parole papers to the governor's desk."

"You mean Donald could actually get paroled?"

A couple of the men laughed. Someone gave a loud snort of contempt.

"Put it this way," said Turk. "They've been doing these risk assessments for the past fifteen years, and so far no lifer's ever gotten parole."

Charles explained. "It's pointless. What going to Patuxent really means is two or three months of misery. Then you're sent back over to wherever you were before."

In just over a year, we'd lost Kevin, Guy, Sig for a while, and now Donald. It was true that other prisoners, equally bright and keen, had taken their places, but every time we lost one of the original nine men, even temporarily, it was a blow to the group's integrity. I'd worked hard to win the men's confidence, and continuity was vital. If it didn't have a solid structure, the book club would seem weak, unreliable, and even unreal.

I was especially curious about how Turk would manage without Donald. Sometimes the pair was like a comedy duo. Donald was the low-key, laconic straight man; Turk was the rambunctious fall guy, roped in as the target of Donald's provocations. They liked to tell me stories about life in C block, "the gated community" where the factory workers lived. Then I remembered that I'd once asked Turk about his "friend," meaning Donald, and Turk had corrected me.

"I got no friends here," he'd said. "Donald is my comrade. We go way back in time and we've been through a lot together."

I realized this was exactly why the men didn't let themselves grow too close. Make friends, and you're setting yourself up for damage. Charles knew the score. Any day, you could wake up and find yourself alone.

Some people think this kind of close human feeling is exactly what's missing in *Dr. Jekyll and Mr. Hyde.* Vladimir Nabokov, who lectured on Stevenson's novel regularly at Cornell, felt there was "no throb in the throat of the story." While he agreed that Jekyll's plight is horrible, Nabokov argued that we don't have the same sense in *Jekyll and Hyde* as we have in Kafka, for instance, of someone struggling to escape from the frame, to break out of the story into the world we inhabit, "to cast off the mask, to transcend the cloak or the carapace."

We began, however, by talking not about Jekyll but about Hyde.

Sig was surprised by the appearance of the doctor's alter ego.

He'd expected someone much bigger. "I thought he'd look like a werewolf, or at least have fangs."

"Me too," said Vincent. "I imagined he'd be like the Incredible Hulk or something."

"The book says he's like a normal guy, except he's smaller than Jekyll," recalled J.D.

J.D. was right. Stevenson describes Hyde as "much smaller, slighter and younger" than Jekyll, who actually feels "lighter, happier in body" when he's wearing the shape of Hyde. He may not be physically repulsive, but still, something about Hyde gives people the creeps. "There is something wrong with his appearance; something displeasing, something downright detestable. I never saw a man I so disliked, and yet I scarce know why," says Mr. Enfield, a relative of Mr. Utterson. "He gives a strong feeling of deformity, although I couldn't specify the point."

"What about Dr. Jekyll? Does he look the way you imagined him?" I asked.

"Which Dr. Jekyll?" asked Steven.

"What do you mean? There's only one."

"There's only one?"

"Sure. Henry Jekyll."

"So who's Harry Jekyll?"

"The same guy. Harry's short for Henry."

"Really? That's crazy," said Steven. "I thought he was, like, Dr. Jekyll's dad or something."

"No, it's a nickname. It's kind of old-fashioned, like calling someone Jack instead of John."

"Wait, Jack's short for John? That's crazy," repeated Steven.

"So now that we've straightened that out," I said, "what did you make of Dr. Jekyll?"

"He seems older than I imagined," said Nick. "In the movies he's always this handsome young guy."

In one part of the novel, Dr. Jekyll is described as "a large, well-made, smooth-faced man of fifty," and in another place, he describes himself as "almost an elderly man."

"Also, when he's Hyde, he looks different on the outside, but he's still Jekyll on the inside," added Sig. "His thoughts don't change. Everything is always from Jekyll's point of view, even when he's Hyde."

"He writes letters and statements and even signs checks as Jekyll," I agreed. "Hyde isn't a separate personality living 'inside' Jekyll; he's just a shape Jekyll sometimes takes on. In the last chapter he says that before he developed the potion, he'd already committed to a 'profound duplicity' of life."

"What's 'duplicity'?" asked Turk.

"It means he's been living a double life, right?" said Steven.

"Right," I said. "Jekyll admits he's always had certain inappropriate desires, and while he didn't used to feel so conflicted about these feelings when he was young, when he started getting older and becoming well-known, they started to get inconvenient. Jekyll doesn't create Hyde by accident, like in the movies. He creates Hyde deliberately, because he wants to do things that a man of his class, age, and position isn't supposed to do."

"I bet it's something sexual. Going to prostitutes, maybe?" suggested Steven.

"No. I think it's drugs. Didn't they all use opium back then?" asked Nick.

"I think it's violence. He kills that old guy and tramples on that little girl," said Turk.

"Must be into S&M," said J.D.

"Sadism, at any rate," I said. "In the last chapter, 'Henry Jekyll's Full Statement of the Case,' he mentions, 'lusting to inflict pain,' and refers to 'torture' and 'depravity.'"

"I think a lot of doctors get off on causing people pain," said Turk.

"Maybe that's why they become doctors," suggested Vincent.

I talked to the men about the concept of sublimation—Freud's idea of a negative impulse being transformed into something more beneficial. Freud came upon the idea, I told the men, after reading about a famous surgeon who, as a child, got pleasure from cutting off dogs' tails.

"But Jekyll hasn't been able to sublimate his sadistic impulses," I reminded them. "It's kind of ironic that he spends his days trying to stop people's pain, and his evenings trying to cause it."

"When you think about the ideas in this book," said Sig, "'good' and 'evil' start to seem inadequate."

"And whatever you can say about Jekyll, you can't say he's not self-aware," I said. "He admits his inappropriate desires. In 'Henry Jekyll's Full Statement of the Case,' he says, 'I was no more myself when I laid aside restraint and plunged in shame, than when I labored, in the eye of day, at the furtherance of knowledge or the relief of sorrow and suffering.' In a way, he's more honest than people who don't tell anybody about their private lives."

"Like guys on the down low," mumbled Day-Day.

"Yeah. Or like all those sleazy politicians who get caught with prostitutes or doing crack or whatever," said Nick.

"Right. If you're in the public eye," I said, "you've got to be really good at compartmentalizing your feelings. People sometimes use the phrase 'a Jekyll-and-Hyde personality' to refer to a

person who has a completely different character from one moment to the next, but actually, Jekyll and Hyde aren't that different. They both have the same mind. Only their bodies are
different."

We went on to talk about how, for Jekyll, compartmentalization never becomes second nature, which is exactly why he needs
Hyde. Some people are experts at splitting off their sexual sides,
for example, never thinking about sex during the day, when
they're at work, or when they're sober; but Jekyll can't relax into
this kind of everyday hypocrisy—not because his conscience is
too strong but because he's too anxious about being discovered.
He's too proud to let go, too concerned about his reputation.
Ironically—for a Victorian, anyway—he suffers from an inability to repress.

I thought about this as I drove back to Baltimore. To some
degree, the more we're able to repress, the more successful we
are. An inability to compartmentalize is one of the main signs
of mental illness. We discuss animal rights over ham sand-
wiches, rail against inequality but ignore the homeless guy asking for change, drive to environmentalist meetings in our SUVs.
Especially in the corporate environment, we're encouraged to
keep our work lives separate from our private lives. We're expected to be strategic rather than intimate in our revelations
and relationships. We're deterred from being too deeply self-
revealing to our workplace colleagues, presenting a version of
ourselves that's neat and professional, that doesn't spill over the
edges, betraying emotional neediness, instability, or desire. If
we can't resist the urge to cry, curse, or pray, we lock ourselves
in our offices—or, as a last resort, a bathroom stall—and let off
steam in private.

I recalled Sergeant Kelly's warnings.

"These men are convicts," she'd informed us, standing at the front of the room with a set of handcuffs and a canister of teargas hanging from her belt. "They're all liars, and they're all manipulators. They'll try to compromise you. You should never forget, these men are dangerous, hardened criminals. They're not your friends." Compartmentalization, I thought, is the soul of the prison, right down to its segregation cells.

Then I thought again. In the outside world, we sleep, play, and work in different places, with different people. In prison, you might very well live with the same people for twenty or thirty years, seeing them every day, at meals, in the shower, in the yard, in the visiting room, in the chapel, in the commissary. In that sense, prison life offers no compartmentalization at all.

Despite Sergeant Kelly's warnings, I did consider the men in the book club to be my friends. Maybe they weren't the kind of friends I could bring home for dinner, but that was only because they weren't allowed to come. Had we met in other circumstances, we may not have been close, but then, I couldn't imagine any other circumstances in which we'd have been brought together. Normally, I rarely venture outside my Baltimore neighborhood. Still, if what Sergeant Kelly said was true and the men did want something from me—even if only my sympathy or my allegiance—that didn't necessarily make them different from anyone else. Everyone's personality is socially adaptive, to some degree. We all make use of one another in all kinds of ways, none of which preclude genuine friendship or even love.

MAY 6, 2014

I kicked things off today by reciting Oscar Wilde's famous line from his essay "The Truth of Masks": "Man is least himself when he talks in his own person. Give a man a mask and he will tell you the truth." We talked about how Wilde's line could be applied to Dr. Jekyll, and our conversation soon came around to the differences between what's permitted today and what was acceptable in Victorian England in 1886. For the most part, the men had a very vague sense of history, and were under the impression that in Stevenson's day, culture was far more repressive than it is today. In some ways this is true, but in other ways, things were—quite literally—far more open. London would have smelled horrible: from sewage dumped in the Thames, horse manure in the streets, and carcasses hanging in butchers' shops, dripping blood onto the sawdust. There was no indoor plumbing, let alone hot water, deodorant, toothpaste, or shampoo. As a physician, Dr. Jekyll would have been familiar with birth, death, and disease, as well as overflowing chamber pots, infected abscesses, botched abortions, and other

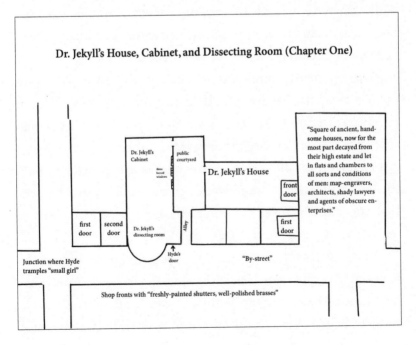

Dr. Jekyll's House, Cabinet, and Dissecting Room (Chapter One)

Dr. Jekyll's Cabinet

public courtyard

three barred windows

Dr. Jekyll's House

front door

"Square of ancient, handsome houses, now for the most part decayed from their high estate and let in flats and chambers to all sorts and conditions of men: map-engravers, architects, shady lawyers and agents of obscure enterprises."

first door

second door

Dr. Jekyll's dissecting room

Alley

first door

Junction where Hyde tramples "small girl"

Hyde's door

"By-street"

Shop fronts with "freshly-painted shutters, well-polished brasses" horrors, including venereal disease—the dark side of sexual freedom. It's not surprising he has trouble keeping things separate.

As we talked, I handed out copies of a diagram I'd made of Dr. Jekyll's premises as Stevenson describes them (and this description is my favorite part of the book). The doctor's house is the second from the corner in a square of "ancient, handsome" buildings. From the front, it has "a great air of wealth and comfort." When you knock, the front door is opened by Poole, the butler, who escorts you into a "large, low-roofed, comfortable hall" paved with flagstones, warmed by an open fire, and "furnished with costly cabinets of oak." Mr. Utterson calls this hall "the pleasantest room in London."

To get to Dr. Jekyll's laboratory, you have to go through the house—"a long journey down two pairs of stairs, through the back passage"—and outside, across an open yard that connects to a small alleyway. Here, facing the house is a stone building with a domed roof that the previous owner, a famous surgeon, had used as his "dissecting room." This contains a small, old-fashioned operating theater, "once crowded with eager students and now lying gaunt and silent . . . the light falling dimly through the foggy cupola." At the far end, a flight of stairs leads to a door covered with red baize. This is the door to Dr. Jekyll's private office or "cabinet," a large room with a fireplace, a chimney, a mirror, and three dusty windows barred with iron (even though they're on the second floor) overlooking the courtyard. Another flight of stairs connects this room to a corridor that leads from the dissecting room to the back street door.

If you walk around the outside of Jekyll's house, behind the handsome façade, you come to a side street at the rear. Walk down this street and you pass the alleyway leading to the courtyard, and "just at that point, a certain sinister block of building thrust forward its gable on the street. It was two stories high; showed no window, nothing but a door on the lower story." This is the back door to the dissecting room—the door that provides the title of the book's first chapter. It's set in a recess and over-hung by a gable; it has a "blind forehead of discoloured wall." It's "sinister," "blistered," and "distained." It's "equipped with nei-ther bell nor knocker, and bears in every feature, the marks of prolonged and sordid negligence." Tramps slouch in the recess and strike matches on the panels. Mr. Enfield has seen Hyde come and go through this entrance, and says, "Black-Mail House is what I call that place with the door." He knows something strange is going on there, but tries to keep out of it.

"I make it a rule of mine," he says. "The more it looks like Queer Street, the less I ask."

"A very good rule too," says the lawyer.

The essential point is that the buildings are connected. They're both elements of Jekyll's premises, necessary parts of the whole, just as his professional healing and his personal sadism are parts of the same personality—perhaps, as Vincent sug-gested, different manifestations of the same impulse. As Mr. En-field puts it, "the buildings are so packed together about that court, that it's hard to say where one ends and another begins." In the same way, Jekyll and Hyde aren't separate identities but one single personality in all its struggling, unruly complexity.

We'd talked at length about Jekyll's dark side. Now I asked the men if they thought there were any good qualities in Hyde.

While we were discussing this question, Nick arrived late. The only seat left in the room, I realized, was a small, pink plas-tic chair that could almost have been designed for a nursery. As he sat down in it, Nick's knees almost reached his chin. If the classroom chairs were too small for Sig, they were way too small for Nick, who was even taller. Could Nick and Sig, I wondered, be XYY males? Men born with an extra male chromosome are always taller than average males. It was once believed that XYY males had a propensity to psychopathy, but there was apparently no evidence to back up this theory. I wondered how Sig and Nick fit into their bunks. I wondered whether their cellmates were pissed to learn they had to share their space with someone who took up rather more than their fair share.

I realized I'd been staring at Nick.

"What do you think, Nick?" I asked him. "Any good qualities in Hyde?"

"Well, he pays off the parents of that little girl he crushes," he said, referring to an incident in which Hyde tramples on a child, leaving her "screaming on the ground."

"Yes, but only so they don't go to the police."

"It's better than nothing," countered Steven.

"And he didn't have to give them a hundred pounds," Nick added. "That was a lot of money in those days. I bet they'd have taken less."

"Also, it's Hyde's choice to turn back into Jekyll. He takes the antidote. He doesn't have to," said Sig.

"He has high-class taste. I guess you could say that's a good quality," Steven pointed out. "Didn't they say his house had really fancy napkins?"

I couldn't remember the passage Steven was referring to, so we looked it up. It's the moment when Utterson discovers that Hyde's house, located in one of London's most dismal slums, is, as Steven recalled, furnished with luxury and good taste. "A closet was filled with wine, the plate was of silver, the napery elegant," we learn, "and the carpets were of many plies and agreeable in colour."

"I think it was probably Jekyll that chose the carpet and all that," Steven added.

I had to agree. I couldn't imagine Mr. Hyde mulling over different shades of tableware.

MAY 12, 2014

By the following week, the Cut—the former Maryland House of Correction—had been completely demolished. The green Italianate cupola and weather vane that once stood on top of the roof now sat on the ground next to a huge pile of bricks and rubble. In between the layers of razor wire, a troop of yellow goslings waddled after their mother in the sunshine.

Inside the prison, the heat was stifling. To make things worse, a pipe had burst somewhere and the water had been cut off. There was nothing to drink, and the toilets wouldn't flush. If the men needed to defecate, they had to either go outside in the yard or use a plastic bag. This had been going on since breakfast time, they told me. Today, the fetid reek of Victorian London didn't seem so far away.

The *Baltimore City Paper* article had come out a few days earlier, and I thought the reporter, Baynard Woods, had done a terrific job. It was the cover story, and continued for eight pages; all in all, it was a well-researched, intelligent, and honest piece of reporting. For legal reasons, the photographer, J. M. Giordano, hadn't been allowed to take pictures of the prisoners' faces. This worked in his favor, as he'd had to find a creative way to photograph them. He'd taken black-and-white pictures of the men's hands and arms—I recognized Steven, Sig, and Day-Day from their tattoos—holding their copies of *Macbeth*. Woods had also conducted an interview with Drew Leder, the philosophy professor who'd started the college program at JCI, and he'd included quotes from this interview as well as some of the dialogue from our class (including, of course, Day-Day's expletives and references to gangs and "pussy").

It's always interesting to see people you know through different eyes, and I was slightly taken aback to find Donald referred to as "the old lifer in the hat." I'd never thought of Donald, who's fifty-three, as being old, nor had I noticed that Turk "stoops a bit as he walks." Day-Day was described as "a young African-American man covered in tattoos, including one between his eyes," and Nick as "an extremely tall white man with a goofy, almost innocent, grin." As for myself, I was likened to the tough, elegant heroine of a Danish crime show. Other than this, the convicts came across just as they were: rough-and-ready but dedicated and eager to learn.

There was only one line that made me uncomfortable. "On the ride back to town through the rain," wrote Woods, "Brottman said the prisoners were on their best behavior for my visit and that normally there was a lot more talk about 'pussy.'" I knew at the time I'd expressed myself badly, and my statement on the page didn't convey the good-humored reference to Day-Day I'd intended. Still, it was a single line hidden inconspicuously in the depths of an exceptionally upbeat and positive eight-page article that I imagined had to be great publicity for the prison and the college program.

The JCI librarian, Grace Schroeder, e-mailed me to say she'd made copies for the men in the reading group. I thought they'd be as thrilled as I was. Yet the first two prisoners I met that day, Charles and Vincent, both had the opposite reaction. In fact, Vincent was angrier than I'd even seen him before.

"I'll never let a reporter here again," he said bitterly.

"Why?" I was stunned. "What's wrong with it?"

"Everything!" Vincent was red in the face. "It completely reinforces the public stereotype of prisoners. For five years I've been fighting with the prison administration to show the importance of these nonaccredited activities. The authorities think they're a waste of time, and they'll use this article to back up their argument. Instead of showing what we've achieved and writing about all the things we've learned, it just reinforces the image we've been battling against: that men in prison are covered with tattoos and they can't have an intelligent conversation without using dirty words."

"But most of the guys *do* have tattoos," I objected. "And Day-Day *did* use those words."

"Right," said Vincent. "But they could have photographed the guys that don't have tattoos. And why did he have to quote Day-Day? Why didn't he quote Charles, or me, or Sig, or any of the other guys who had intelligent things to say? Everyone who reads this is going to think, 'Typical: Give them a female instructor and all they can talk about is pussy.' They'll think we don't know how to behave appropriately in a classroom setting. It's like doing an interview on slavery in the 1800s and saying all blacks talk about is returning to the jungle."

"Everyone I've spoken to about it has been so impressed," I argued, feeling mortified by my own contribution to the scandal. "They can't believe you guys are reading Conrad and Melville and Shakespeare. Ms. Schroeder liked it. Even the media relations guy from the Department of Corrections liked it, and his job is dealing with publicity."

"Doesn't matter," insisted Vincent. "The only thing that matters to us is what the authorities in *this* prison think of it. They'll find a way to use it against us, you wait and see."

"The fact is, Day-Day shouldn't have been using that kind of language," Charles joined in. "If you're at a family dinner, or at church, at a job interview, or in a place of education, you don't talk that way."

"But Day-Day's never been in one of those situations. And anyway, we're not in church or at a family dinner; we're in a prison," I said, highly conscious that both Charles and Vincent were politely refraining from mentioning the language *I'd* used.

"When I was at Patuxent," continued Charles, "one man got drunk and didn't come back from his work release. Long story short, we all lost our work release status because of him. One prisoner can screw everything up for the rest of us. If somebody in administration or custody finds out there's a group in here led by a female where Day-Day's kind of language is tolerated, they'd cancel it immediately. I know how custody thinks. Plus, it's just ignorant. It's not necessary to cuss in every sentence. Out of respect, I very rarely cuss when I'm talking to my wife, and during your classes I feel the same way about cussing in front of you."

"It's an eight-page article," I insisted, starting to feel sick with guilt. "Eight pages of small print. Three thousand words, and it's all incredibly positive except for that one single line."

"Imagine a bucket of water," said Charles, always ready with an analogy. "It could be the purest water from the purest mountain stream, but you add one tiny little drop of poison, and the whole rest of the water's tainted, and anybody who drinks it will die."

He was right. I'm sure Charles didn't remember the lines, but Macbeth says something very similar in Act II, Scene II, lines 61–64, when he looks down at his hands after murdering the king:

Will all great Neptune's ocean wash this blood
Clean from my hand? No, this my hand will rather
The multitudinous seas incarnadine,
Making the green one red.

My crime wasn't of the same magnitude, but Charles and Vincent's anger made me feel just as guilty as Macbeth. I desperately wanted to change the subject.

"How's your eye, Charles?" I asked him.

"Real uncomfortable," he grumbled. "My right eye works normally, but my left eye doesn't, so everything looks blurry. If I could make some kind of eye patch or something to cover it, I'd be able to see, but I've got nothing to make one from."

"That's horrible," I said as the other men began to arrive. A moment later Charles reached for his Styrofoam cup of water. His arm was shaking, and he accidentally knocked it over. Sig, who'd just arrived, went to get some paper towels to help clean up the spill. When he got back, I watched him mop up the water carefully. Then I saw him put an arm around the older man's shoulder.

"How you doing, Chuck?" he asked. "Everything OK?"

It was the first time I'd seen one of the men show genuine kindness to another, and it made a deep impression on me.

The other men all wanted to know what I thought of the *City Paper* article. Now I was afraid and on my guard.

"What about you guys?" I said apprehensively. "Tell me what you thought of it."

"I loved it," said Steven. That was no surprise. But to my great relief, so did Sig, Nick, Turk, J.D., and Day-Day. They were thrilled to see photographs of their tattoos in the newspaper and asked me if I could bring in extra copies for them to give to their friends. In fact, after a long debate, even Vincent conceded that not everybody would see the piece the way he saw it.

"I suppose it could be enlightening for some people," he confessed finally. "I sent a copy to my sister, and I've got to admit, she thought it was pretty cool."

8

"THE BLACK CAT"

I spent my sixteenth summer absorbed in *The Illustrated Edgar Allan Poe*, a handsome hardback from the local library edited by Roy Gasson and published by Jupiter Books in 1976. This volume contained not only Poe's most opulent stories but also the work of his best-known illustrators: Arthur Rackham, Harry Clarke, Gustave Doré, Édouard Manet, W. Heath Robinson, and Aubrey Beardsley. (I admired the dreamy, sinuous Heath Robinson angels, but always preferred Beardsley's decadent grotesques.) Poe's portrait was the book's frontispiece, and I found him darkly, dreamily handsome despite his high forehead and receding hair. His gloomy stories enchanted my life, and I read them hungrily, thoughtlessly. Many of them were long and difficult, but I struggled on regardless, partly because I had nothing else to do.

Now, walking to work in the morning with my dog, I pass a statue of Poe, his head tilted slightly, his left hand raised. The author's former Baltimore residence on North Amity Street—a tiny three-room brick row house—has been turned into a museum. The attic room, with a writing desk by the window, is so cramped you have to stoop to get in the door. It's easy to see how this claustrophobic space could have inspired escapist fantasies, especially of premature burial. The horrors endured in this house weren't Gothic nightmares but the same ordinary, bleak ordeals that many of the prisoners have to deal with: poverty, neglect, disease, and addiction from which Poe took refuge at his attic writing desk, in his flights of lugubrious fancy.

Or so the story goes. In fact, no one knows whether the desk in the Edgar Allan Poe House is Poe's actual desk, which room he used to write in, or even how much of the house is the original structure. This uncertainty, combined with its location in a notoriously dodgy neighborhood ("Go here if u want to get shot," writes one visitor on Yelp.com) meant the Poe House was never high on the list of Baltimore's tourist attractions and lost its financing in September 2012. A month after it was shut down, the house was defaced by graffiti and someone made off with its wooden front steps. Since then it's resurfaced under the guise of a new nonprofit organization, Poe Baltimore, Inc., but is open to visitors only on weekends. The memorial's poverty seems a sad extension of the author's destitution.

JUNE 4, 2014

The first prisoner I recognized on the compound was Donald. He was waiting for me by the fence, looking hot and tired from a long morning's labor in the woodshop. A damp gray towel hung around his neck, and a pair of sunglasses sat on the gleaming bald dome of his head.

I was thrilled to see him. "Hey! I thought they'd be keeping you at Patuxent for months."

"Nope. I got lucky. They sent me back after thirty-six days." He appeared simultaneously pleased to be back and angry at being taken away in the first place. As we walked down the hall together, he filled me in on his thirty-six-day "vacation."

"Soon as I get there, right, they put me through the strip-search procedure, then they handcuff me and put me in administrative segregation. They say, 'You're considered a danger to the security of the institution, convicts, and staff.' Ten days later they come and tell me it's all been a mistake. They've got the wrong guy. I tell them, 'Well, somebody knows why this happened. Somebody wrote down my name. Somebody came and shackled me and put me in a van.' They said it was an 'administrative mix-up.' That was after ten days. I could have come back here right then, but they'd put some other guy in my cell already. The other twenty-six days I was just waiting for an empty cell."

"I thought they sent you for a psych evaluation." I remembered Donald had once told me that, although all the material things he owned would fit into two trash bags, he'd probably need at least two more to carry around all his "mentalistic bullshit." In this light, it hadn't seemed out of the question that someone in authority might want to know what was going on inside that shining dome of his.

"Psych had nothing to do with it," he said. "Don't know who sent me. All I know is I never want to go there again. You know the cells in Patuxent, right?"

"No," I said. "I've never been there."

"They're like dog cages. Man, I can't stand that place."

"You don't think it was an 'administrative mix-up'?"

DONALD

"Are you serious? Everything in here happens because somebody wants it to happen."

"So somebody wanted to teach you a lesson?" We entered the classroom and, as usual, J.D.'s dog, Falcon, rushed over to greet me, wagging his tail furiously and doing his best to stick his snout up my skirt. I'd learned how to pet him and fend him off at the same time.

"Oh, I got enemies all right," said Donald, lowering himself tenderly into his usual chair. (Two slipped disks in his back were the cause of constant pain.) "I got plenty of enemies. They think I'm dangerous. And at one time they were right. I used to be a time bomb waiting to go off. Thing is, I'm not like that right now. I've found my comfort zone and I've got some positive things going on. This book club is very good for me, to be honest. Keeps me out of trouble. I've got something to focus on: doing the reading and putting in the work. And making sure these other fuckups do the same."

Maybe I'm cynical, but I assumed the men said exactly the same thing to all the prison volunteers. Most of the men were practiced manipulators, after all. But in Donald's case I really believed he was speaking from the heart, because he was normally so truculent and laconic. Or perhaps the special impact of his words had something to do with the bond between us. With some of the men—Steven, Charles, and Vincent, for example—I was openly friendly, and we'd often chat about our lives and those of our families and friends. My pact with Donald was different. It was deep but unexpressed. We shared the same dark view of life. The prisoners often teased me about my pessimism, my taste for black clothes and "depressing" literature. But Donald shared my darkness. He put me in mind of a line spoken by the good-natured Razumihin in Fyodor Dostoyevsky's *Crime and Punishment*: "To go wrong in one's own way is better than to go right in someone else's."

Donald was doing a life sentence for armed robbery and murder; he also had convictions for battery, false imprisonment, theft, and possession of drugs. He told me he'd been "labeled a sociopath by judge and jury." When I asked if he wanted me to write a letter to the parole board on his behalf—the first time I'd ever made such an offer without being asked—he simply shrugged and replied, "There's no point. I'm facing life plus a hundred years."

Eventually, the rest of the prisoners arrived: Charles, wearing an eye patch and looking a little less drained than usual; Sig, his beard due for a trim; Nick, eager to talk about the World Cup.

"Do you think England will win?" he asked me.

"No chance," I said, shaking my head.

"Everyone thinks I want the U.S. to win just because I live here," Nick informed me, "but me and Sig want England to win. England or Germany."

"And what about Steven?"

"He's an Italy fan. But he's going to miss most of the games. He's on lockup."

"Really?"

"Yeah. The CO found a needle inside his cellmate's shoe. Steve didn't know anything about it. But there's a rule that if they find contraband in your cell, both you and your cellmate get punished. It's supposed to be a deterrent. They don't believe one guy can have contraband in his cell without his cellmate knowing."

"That's too bad," I said. "Steven would have liked Edgar Allan Poe."

"Yeah. Steven likes everything," said Nick.

As it turned out, of all the prisoners, only Vincent was already familiar with the work of Poe. Some of the other men recognized the author's name, but only in connection with the Ravens, Baltimore's football team, and so the whole of our first meeting was spent discussing the author's life and death. There was a lot to talk about.

I explained Poe's connection to Baltimore, which, to me, has always seemed a bit of a stretch. He was born in Boston in 1809, lived for five years in London, went to college in Virginia, and spent the next twenty-four years moving between Richmond, Philadelphia, and New York, where he lived at nine different addresses and wrote most of his best-known works. He moved to Baltimore in 1833 and lived in the city until sometime in 1835, at which point he moved back to Richmond with his young cousin and bride. Like many things in the author's life, his death and burial in Baltimore seem to have been a mistake: the consensus view is that he was trying to get to New York from Philadelphia but took the wrong train by mistake. Nobody knows exactly what happened then—though theories abound, and the prisoners, when I told them the story, had plenty of their own—but the poet was found delirious in a street outside a Baltimore tavern on October 3, 1849, and died four days later.

JUNE 11, 2014

I handed out photocopies of "The Black Cat," which is my favorite of Poe's stories, although I'm not exactly sure why. While it's short, it's also forceful and complicated, and I wanted to take it slowly. The tale is told by an unnamed narrator—most of the men assumed, naturally enough, that this was Poe himself—who begins by informing us that the circumstances he's about to describe are "a series of mere household events." As a child, he was gentle and tenderhearted. "I was especially fond of animals, and was indulged by my parents with a great variety of pets." But during the course of the story we come to see how the narrator's special fondness for animals, an otherwise healthy human impulse, becomes increasingly tainted by an obsessive fear and hatred. For reasons unknown he's tormented by an overwhelming sense of self-disgust that he tries—unsuccessfully—to repress. He finds relief in alcohol, and when he's drunk, he aims his destructive urges at those around him: first his cat and then his wife.

We read and discussed the first half of the story, stopping at a point where the narrator is startled to see the image of a cat with a noose around its neck in the ruins of his house, which has just burned to the ground. Somebody, he thinks, must have thrown the dead cat through his bedroom window in a desperate attempt to wake him up.

"That's crazy," said Donald. "He's starting to lose it."

Vincent disagreed. "You know," he said, "they do that in some prisons, I heard."

"Do what?" I asked.

"Throw dead cats inside."

"Why would anybody do that?" I asked him.

"To get cell phones into the prison. They sew them up inside a dead cat," said Vincent.

"I don't get it. Why a dead cat?"

"Who knows?" Vincent shrugged casually. "Just something I heard."

"They a lot of cats around here," said Day-Day.

"Back in the day, they used to let feral cats live in the penitentiary to keep the rat population down," continued Vincent.

"Once we found these two kittens in the bottom of the elevator shaft. I took one of them back to my cell and kept her as a pet. I called her Spud. I gave her milk with an eyedropper until she could eat solid food, then I gave her tuna from the kitchen. I had that cat for quite a few years. I built shelves in my cell so she could jump around and play on them, and I left the TV on for her when I went to work. She had a pretty good life for a cat."

"What happened to her?"

"She made parole." Vincent grinned. "I decided she'd done enough time, so I sent her home to my mother. We had a big party for her. I still have a picture of the two of us in the visiting room with this big sign we made: 'Spud Makes Parole.'"

"Now, if Poe had written that story, it wouldn't have had such a happy ending," I said.

"Oh, you should hear about my other cats," said Vincent. "They didn't have happy endings. The first cat I had, a CO slammed a door on him. Killed him right in front of my eyes."

"Oh, my God," I gasped. "That's horrible!"

"Well, he said it was an accident. Whatever." Vincent waved a hand in dismissal. "Anyway, I got another one. In those days, quite a few of the guys kept stray cats in their cells. So one day the assistant warden decides 'No more cats.' We had to round them all up and get rid of them. At nine in the morning the CO tells us we've got to call somebody on the outside to come and pick up our cats, and if they haven't been picked up by two in the afternoon they'll be sent to the SPCA. Most of the guys don't have anyone to call. I call my mother, but she's at work, she can't just drop everything and drive over to the prison. She says, 'Don't worry, Vinnie. I'll go and pick him up before work tomorrow morning from the SPCA.' They said the cats would be put up for adoption, but they lied to us. They were killed as soon as they got to the SPCA. When my mother got there, he was already dead."

As Vincent spoke, it crossed my mind that at least on this occasion my words in the *City Paper* were vindicated: today the men really did want to talk about nothing but pussy. I also realized that it had stopped bothering me when the men got off topic like this. We may have been going somewhere we didn't plan to go, but we were still going somewhere.

I handed out copies of the two illustrations that had accompanied "The Black Cat" in my *Illustrated Edgar Allan Poe*. The first, by Harry Clarke, shows the corpse of the narrator's wife as it's described in Poe's story, "already greatly decayed and clotted with gore." Draped around the cadaver's shoulders is a huge cat, grinning with malice. Much as I loved this image, I found the second even more compelling. Aubrey Beardsley's enormous black cat is a one-eyed, muscle-bound demon, and in this rendition the narrator's dead wife is dolled up in an evening dress and has a shroud of white hair like an eighteenth-century wig.

"So, did this really happen to Edgar Allan Poe?" asked Turk as the men studied the two illustrations. "And if not, what made him think up such a weird-ass story?"

"It didn't actually happen to Poe, but some people do think it's based on a real guy," I told him. "His name was John Ward. He was a famous cat poisoner."

"Huh," grunted Turk.

Ward's case is mentioned briefly by the Philadelphia physician Benjamin Rush in his series of sixteen lectures on the "murdering impulse," which Poe is known to have read. Sir John Ward was a member of the British Parliament in the eighteenth century who apparently found great pleasure in poisoning cats and watching their painful convulsions as they died. Such instances of depravity, wrote Dr. Rush, do not belong to the ordinary character of man. "They are as much the effects of morbid idiosyncrasy, as a relish for fetid odors, or putrid meats, is of the same states of the senses of smell and taste."

When I first read this case study, I found myself wondering: Am I morbidly idiosyncratic? I can't bear to see an animal in pain. Nor have I—unlike most of the prisoners—ever experienced a "murdering impulse." But I do love Poe's nasty little tales, and I have to confess that my favorite part of "The Black Cat" is the moment when the cat gets under the irritable narrator's feet. He lifts up his ax to kill it and, at the last minute, murders his wife instead: "I withdrew my arm from her grasp and buried the axe in her brain. She fell dead upon the spot, without a groan."

When I got home that evening, I typed the phrase, "dead cats cellphones prison" into Google and found a news story that described how prison authorities at Phillips State Prison in Buford, Georgia, had recently found a dead cat stuffed with eight cell phones that someone had tried to throw over the prison fence.

JUNE 18, 2014

I got to the prison early, and our classroom was empty. Jeffrey, one of the trainee service dogs, was in the corner, cooped up in his cage. It was so hot in the room, and Jeffrey seemed so eager to play, I couldn't help opening his cage and letting him out for a while. As we were playing, a young African-American guy came into the room, introduced himself to me as Johnson, and asked how he could join the book club. Prisoners asked me this all the time, and I always gave them the same answer: Talk to Vincent.

"Well, I got to finish my GED first, I guess," Johnson sighed. "I'm taking a basic math class down the hall."

We chatted for a while as we threw a ball around for Jeffrey. I told Johnson about my new puppy, Oliver, and Johnson told me about the pit bulls he'd kept when he lived "uptown." A lot of the prisoners had kept pit bulls on the outside. Not long ago, one of them had shown me a grimy Polaroid of an angry-looking beast, snarling and slavering, chained up in the backyard of what was clearly a slum. It seemed obvious this dog was kept for fighting, although I don't know if I could have proven it.

"Well, so long, Miss Lady," said Johnson when Vincent and some of the other men arrived. "I gotta go."

After Johnson had left, Vincent warned me I should put Jeffrey back in his cage because Jeffrey's trainer, a guy who went by the name of Baltimore, would be there any minute. I led the reluctant dog back into his own prison, where he sat scratching himself unhappily. Five minutes later, Baltimore, a dapper-looking man in his fifties, came to pick him up.

"Would you mind showing me what Jeffrey can do?" I asked.

"Sure," said Baltimore, and proudly put Jeffrey through his paces, instructing him to sit, lie down, roll over, trace a figure eight, balance a treat on his nose, and even climb into a chair and sit down like a human being. By the time he'd finished, the other men had arrived, rewarding Jeffrey with a hearty round of applause.

They'd come prepared for the heat, with their plastic water bottles filled from the drinking fountain in the hall. Their exercise books, on which most of them had written their names in large letters, were carried in string laundry bags, along with the photocopy I'd made for them of "The Black Cat." Charles was absent: he had another appointment with the eye doctor. Steven was still on lockup. Day-Day sloped into the room, scratched himself, slumped down in his seat, and pulled up his pants. Nick and Sig were even more tanned than they'd been the week before; they'd obviously been playing soccer out in the yard. JCI had a number of different sports teams, including soccer, volleyball, handball, and basketball. At one time I'd have imagined prison to be an unlikely place for team sports to thrive, since they require perseverance and cooperation, but now I knew these were qualities in which many of the prisoners excelled.

We soon finished "The Black Cat." Turk was reading aloud when he came to the narrator's "accidental" murder of his wife, which pulled him up short.

"Hell," he exclaimed, "I wasn't expecting that!"

Donald read the part in which the narrator wonders what to do with her corpse, eventually deciding to wall it up in the cellar, "as the monks of the middle ages are recorded to have walled up their victims." In doing so, he also walls up "the hideous beast," which, he feels, has "seduced" him into murder," and which now betrays him with "a wailing shriek, half of horror and half of triumph."

"This guy's insane," declared Sig when we came to the end of the story. "He's trying to claim the cat made him kill his wife. No jury's going to buy that."

"Depends on his attorney," said Nick. As the conversation continued, I couldn't help recalling Nick's own case, and in particular the description Nick gave to his friend of how he'd placed Danny's body into a hole in the ground.

"I think this guy's got more problems than he realizes," said Donald.

"He got away with it until he told on himself. That damn cat was his guilty conscience," said Turk.

"You know what," said Day-Day, with a slight curl of his upper lip. "I think Turk's got it right. I think he wanted to get caught."

This made a great transition to the reading I'd brought along to help advance our understanding of "The Black Cat." This was Poe's short story (it's really more of a philosophical essay) "The Imp of the Perverse." I read out a few of the most important paragraphs and summarized its content. The narrator, I told the men, begins by boasting that he's managed to commit the perfect crime: a murder that's brought him a large fortune, which he's enjoyed for many years. One day, however, out of nowhere, he starts muttering to himself the words "I am safe—I am safe—yes—if I be not fool enough to make open confession!" The moment this thought comes to mind, apparently out of nowhere, he starts to panic. He can't stop thinking about the possibility that he might be stupid enough to confess. Finally this compulsion gets a grip on him, and despite himself he rushes madly through the heavily populated streets to confront the authorities, in whose presence "some invisible fiend, I thought, struck me with his broad palm upon the back," and "the long imprisoned secret" bursts forth from his soul.

This spirit of self-injury seems to emerge fully formed from the ghostly borderland between waking daylight and the world of dreams. I read the men a brief, key passage from the essay. "With certain minds, under certain conditions, it becomes absolutely irresistible . . . It is a radical, a primitive impulse—elementary." Yet, as I told the men, "the perverse" in this essay doesn't necessarily mean that which we know to be wrong. After all, confessing you've committed a crime is the right thing to do, morally speaking. In "The Imp of the Perverse," wrong isn't wrong for moral or ethical reasons but because it is damaging to the personality who initiates the action. In other words, the "perverse" is whatever goes against the grain of our rational interest and better judgment.

Now that I'm more familiar with Poe's philosophical works, I've found a new depth in his better-known horror stories. Rereading his creepy tales, I often find—as I do with *Heart of Darkness*—something vital in a phrase, moment, or detail I'd previously dismissed as tangential or irrelevant. I now understand that "The Black Cat"—written two years before "The Imp of the Perverse"—is a trying on of the same idea in a fictional form. When he asks himself why he hanged his cat Pluto, the narrator of "The Black Cat" realizes he did so *"because* I knew that it had loved me, and *because* I felt that it had given me no reason of offence." He killed it, he acknowledges, in the teeth of his better judgment. He declares: "It was this unfathomable longing of the soul *to vex itself*—to offer violence to its own nature—to do wrong for wrong's sake only—that urged me to continue and finally to consummate the injury I had inflicted upon the unoffending brute."

As another example of this kind of "perverseness," I told the men how Poe chose his former enemy Rufus Wilmot Griswold to be his literary executor. In Poe's obituary, Griswold notoriously tarnished the dead man's reputation by misquoting his letters and stressing his drunkenness.

Of all the men in the group, it was Day-Day who seemed immediately to understand this impulse, just as he'd seemed to grasp Macbeth's vacillating nature. He even had his own name for it: "backwardness."

"So instead of asking some dude who'd say all these fine things about him," said Day-Day about Poe's obituary, "he chose some guy who told all the bad shit, the real shit."

Everyone in the group could think of "perverse" things they'd said, done, or witnessed in others. I told them about a college friend of mine in England who'd been subject to sudden irrational urges, unpredictable even to himself. One time, I told the men, he was on a train, standing in the area between carriages where you were allowed to smoke in those days, and he found himself staring at the emergency alarm, a red cord running along the carriage roof. Suddenly he felt an urge to pull it. The next thing he knew, the train was screeching to a halt and the guard was running toward him down the aisle, blowing his whistle. My friend apologized at great length, explaining he didn't know what came over him. Surprisingly, his impulse was forgiven. (Perhaps the guard was personally acquainted with the imp of the perverse.) I also told them about a rare neurological condition I'd read about called "alien hand syndrome" in which your hand develops "a life of its own" and tries to unbutton your clothes, to fight your other hand, and even to choke you while you're asleep.

"That's like this thing called the Yips," said J.D. "These guys, these top athletes, they just lose their ability to do something that's always been really easy. Like, a golf player will suddenly lose his swing for no reason, or a baseball player just won't be able to hit the ball. They've never found a reason for it."

"Or it's like when you always fuck up with women because some part of you don't want to be attached," said Day-Day.

"Or when you come out of jail, and you swear you're never going back there again, and then the next thing you know you're standing in front of the judge," said Donald. "That's what happened to me."

It must have been a long time ago. Donald had been in prison for more than thirty years, nineteen of them at JCI. Paradoxi-cally, along with the other older guys in the group, he often spoke nostalgically about the way things used to be in prison— not just at JCI, but in general—before things got "soft." Things had changed, the long-timers complained, over the last fifteen years. "Back in the day," before the introduction of female COs, before men were allowed to have televisions and video games in their cells, things had been tough. And some of the older men seemed to miss those days.

"There was no time for games," Donald would say. "You had to grow up quick."

Like Turk, Charles, and the other older prisoners, Donald had what he referred to as a "prison mind-set," yet found himself sur-rounded by men with an "institutional mind-set." He com-plained that the men around him had allowed themselves to be assimilated, accepting things they'd never have put up with ten years ago. In the old days, he lamented, prisoners would stick together to the death. They were men at war against their life-long enemies, the guards. Now, he felt, things were too easy. Prisoners would fraternize with COs, hoping to win their friend-ship, especially if they were female. There was no "us versus them" anymore. According to Donald, the war was over, and the prison authorities had won.

As a result, Donald told me, he was regarded as a loner, ostra-cized from JCI society. Yet, for a loner, I found him surprisingly popular and easygoing. When I'd given Vincent my slide show to set up for the psychology class, Vincent secretly inserted Don-ald's photo under the heading "The Psychopathic Personality." He knew Donald could take the joke. But I also knew Donald had been in serious trouble. In the same slide show, I'd included

images of Victorian lunatic asylums and the old-fashioned restraints they used. One of the slides showed a picture of what
looked like a pair of lace-up boxing gloves.

Donald recognized them. "Those are mesh mitts," he told
me. "I've worn them many times. They still use them at the supermax. If you get caught masturbating in front of the female
COs, you get a choice: you can wear the mesh mitts for a day or
get a citation."

JUNE 25, 2014

I'd missed Steven. In his absence the book club lacked the special
added energy only he could bring. This week he was back from
the lockup and seemed determined to make up for lost time. His
hair had grown long on top, and even though he'd only got out
the day before, he was already tanned from a day of soccer in the
yard. Naturally he was pissed at the way he'd been treated, yet he
was so pleased to be back he couldn't seem to stop smiling.

"I was in the lockup for twenty-five days, six hours, and forty-
three minutes!" He grinned. "For nothing! While you guys were
reading Edgar Allan Poe. I've always wanted to read Edgar Allan
Poe! And I missed all the World Cup games! I got out just in time
to see Italy lose to Uruguay, and I was so pissed. Italy's my team.
It's not fair, man. None of it's fair." Still smiling, he took his usual
seat on my left and started telling me about what conditions were
like in the lockup, and what he'd had to eat, and how the COs
had treated him. There was a lot of laughing and joking around,
and although I wanted to find out whether he'd had a chance to
read the story, I was also enjoying the pleasure of having Steven
back again. He laughed so easily, and his laugh seemed so genuine, that he always made me laugh too. What's more, by now I

knew the kinds of things that made him laugh—reminding him of the way Guy's pants always used to hang halfway down his butt, for example, or recalling Day-Day's "pussy" letter—and I couldn't help saying things I knew would set him off.

I can't say laughing was something I expected to do much of in a maximum security prison, but I laughed more in the book club than I've done since I was a kid. I laughed in ways I hadn't laughed for so long, I hardly recognized them: sudden, undignified snorts; irrepressible sniggers; the kind of laughter that made my stomach hurt. I was reminded of the kind of joy that came from being absorbed in a group, with its exuberant and irrepressible energy.

"Did you get a chance to read the story?" I asked Steven when he finally shut up.

"I sure did," he said, "though after twenty-five days in the lockup, to be honest with you, I really didn't want to read about somebody being walled up in a basement. I mean, OK, the lady was dead, but the cat was still alive. I didn't want to think about it. That's about the worst thing that can happen, to be buried alive."

"Oh, yeah?" countered Donald. "You think so? Better to be buried alive and die from suffocation or starvation or whatever than be buried alive for thirty-five, forty years, like some of the guys in here." His tirades against the system always generated murmurs of agreement from the men, and echoes of "That's right" from his comrade Turk, who in this instance was nodding eagerly, his glasses starting to slide down his nose, as they tended to do when he got animated.

"Even if that cat was evil, it didn't deserve to be buried alive," Vincent affirmed. "But they bury us alive without thinking twice about it."

"When the state does it, it's not even questioned," added Donald.

Murmurs of agreement followed. But others resisted the polemic, wanting the chance to address other aspects of the story. Nick, who often struck me as a bit cocky himself, was fascinated by the narrator's arrogance.

"This guy's way too confident," he said. "He thinks he's got away with it. That's why he starts tapping on the walls when the police are there."

"This guy reminds me of some of the DC and Baltimore killers a few of us here grew up with," said Turk. "These guys are slick, and some of them are mad, like this guy, but even when they're crazy, they're smooth operators. This story is pretty realistic. I've known guys who would do something like this."

"Me too," Donald said, nodding.

"I think that's why my wife didn't want to hear this one," said Turk. "Usually we read these stories together over the phone and talk about them. But with this one, when we got to the part where the guy hits his wife in the head with an ax, Sharon interrupts me. She goes, 'This is too morbid. I don't want to hear any more.' I don't think she like this Mr. Edgar Allan Poe."

"Maybe she got a point," murmured Donald.

9

THE METAMORPHOSIS

I'd writhed and squirmed when I first tried to read *The Metamorphosis*. If *Heart of Darkness* had seemed too complicated, *The Metamorphosis* had seemed too simple. Kafka's language, translated into modern English, had felt uncomfortably matter-of-fact. I think what made me so uneasy was that the world I was reading about reminded me of the world I was living in, and I didn't like it. Kafka was too contemporary for me. I didn't find *The Metamorphosis* interesting at first. On the one hand, I thought I understood it all too well; on the other hand, I didn't understand it at all. It was a long time before I began to appreciate and enjoy this paradox.

JULY 2, 2014

It was way over 90 degrees outside, and the prison classroom felt dank and humid with sweat. The smell of rancid trash drifted in from the hall. A fly buzzed around languidly. At the men's request, I'd brought them a picture of my French bulldog puppy, Oliver. I was surprised how curious they seemed to be about this small creature with his flat snout and big ears.

Day-Day in particular seemed transfixed. He stared at the picture of Oliver for a long time.

"I love him," he concluded.

I loved Oliver, too, and I felt guilty about leaving him when he was still only six months old. I'd kiss him good-bye right before I left for the prison, and all afternoon I'd recall the soft sensation of his damp snout, the faint taste of peanut butter in his wrinkles. Although Oliver was young, he was very well behaved. I'd bring him to my college classes and he'd lie contentedly between my feet, chewing on a treat and making sweet little snorting noises, totally absorbed. It was very painful for me to leave him behind, and I felt slightly resentful that I couldn't bring him with me to the prison.

Nick, Sig, and Steven were still talking excitedly about the World Cup. Steven was wearing a sweatband on his head and a T-shirt printed with "The Nobles," the name of his volleyball team, which consisted of men from the Noble Hearth. Not all prisoners had caught the sun, however. Vincent, who worked indoors, remained pale. So did Charles, despite being employed as the prison window cleaner and general goose-shit wiperupper. He might even have been off work, since he was still wearing his eye patch, and I recalled him recently mentioning that the antibiotics he'd been taking for his cellulitis had been giving him nausea.

I handed out the Dover Thrift Edition of *The Metamorphosis and Other Stories*, translated by Stanley Applebaum. (The "other

stories" were "The Judgment," "In the Penal Colony," "A Country Doctor," and "A Report to an Academy," all of which I encouraged the men to read in their own time.) I gave them a brief
introduction to the life and work of Kafka then we opened *The
Metamorphosis* and began to read, taking it in turn, as usual.

Whenever I asked them to read aloud, most of the prisoners
spoke slowly. Some of them struggled with each line, even with
each word. When this had happened with more challenging
books like *Heart of Darkness* and "Bartleby," I'd sympathized with
their labors; but today I found myself growing impatient, even
wondering if I should put us all out of our misery by reading the
first chapter myself. To me, Kafka's style seemed purposefully
straightforward, and as I sat listening to one man after another
grow tongue-tied, losing his place, stumbling over simple
phrases, and swallowing his words in stodgy mouthfuls, I could
feel myself starting to get exasperated.

It wasn't so much the pace of the men's reading that bothered
me as their inability to look ahead. They'd focus on each word in
the context of the line or, at the very most, the sentence. Everything was in the moment for them. As soon as their turn was
over, their focus would visibly relax, and while they may have
carried on listening, I could tell they weren't always following. I
was astonished that, from week to week, some of the men would
forget the names of characters, essential plot elements, and even
the titles of the books themselves and their authors, if they'd
ever known them to begin with. A couple of the men vaguely
remembered having read *The Metamorphosis* before, in a philosophy class; but apart from the fact that a guy turned into a bug,
they recalled nothing about it, not even the title. Sometimes I felt
depressed to think the books we read made so little impression

on the men. On the other hand, I knew books could have an indiscernible, even unconscious impact, whether or not you remembered their titles.

Listening to the prisoners straining to articulate unfamiliar words, I couldn't help thinking about the way I read, just as learning a second language can alert us to the structure of our native tongues. I learned to read quickly, easily, and almost unconsciously, at a very young age. When reading now, I'll instinctively acknowledge the importance of particular words and ideas, associating them with earlier moments or expressions in the story. The prisoners, on the other hand, had little background in literature, and many of them didn't read a great deal, if at all, apart from magazines and religious texts. They had to make sense of every story as it unfolded, word by word, fitting together each sentence as it appeared before them, with no eye for the future and no time for the past.

Turk seemed to be having special problems with one passage, and as I listened to him stutter and stumble, I was reminded of the way I play the piano. Even though I've been playing for years, whenever I start to learn a piece of music I've never heard before, I have to wrestle with every bar, slowly repeating each phrase, stopping to correct myself every time I play a wrong note, struggling to get to a point where I can start to discern the melody. If I work on a piece every day for twenty minutes, it can still be a week before it's recognizable, even to me, and at least two weeks before I can "play" it. It's a battle that demands my full attention. When David plays, however, I can immediately recognize the difference between my kind of ongoing, in-the-moment struggle and his fluent, natural awareness of how the whole piece works.

But a slow pace and deep concentration can have its own rewards. Although *The Metamorphosis* was perfectly accessible to me, the older I get, the more I find in it, as seems to be the case with so many other books I've returned to at a later date. At the prison, because we went over the first section so slowly and in so much detail, I started to realize that Gregor, when he's transformed, sees everything very differently. For the first time he has the ability to look at the world closely and with sustained attention, and to notice particular details. His bug's-eye view provides enough distance and perspective to make ordinary life appear uncanny.

The familiarity of Gregor's life was also something I'd never really paid close attention to before—or perhaps I should say that the prisoners made me understand how a normal, everyday routine can be, at the same time, an almost unbearable obligation. "It was half past six, and the hands were quietly moving forwards," observes Gregor with great anguish when he first wakes up, having set his alarm clock for four o'clock in the morning. I thought of the prisoners being woken up at four or five or six and having to dress and stand in line for showers and breakfast. I also thought of the young Franz Kafka waking up to the mundane affairs of his life: everyday problems at home and at work, domestic matters, financial anxieties, and health complaints, not to mention the tedious nature of his employment—negotiating workers' insurance claims.

I wondered: Is this how we all live? Do we all have a conscious, interior stream of thought running alongside our public life, or do some of us have only one open, outward existence the way Oliver seems to? You sometimes hear it said of a person that they are "superficial," that they "have no inner life." Is such a thing really possible? If so, might not this kind of life be preferable to the one we're more familiar with? What if intelligence leads not to a higher quality of existence but to neurosis, stress, and disquiet? We assume that animals and insects are insensitive to the finer elements of human culture, but I have no doubt that Oliver's here-and-now existence gives him more pleasure than I get by constantly fretting about tomorrow. Similarly, Gregor's sensitive response to the music his sister plays on her violin ("Was he an animal if music could captivate him so?") serves only to remind him of the human life he's missing. He's much better off when he forgets about music and learns to enjoy insect behavior more suitable to his new state of being ("He was especially fond of hanging from the ceiling; it was quite different from lying on the floor; he could breathe more freely; his body had a light swing to it . . .").

The prisoners were struck by the fact that everyone in the Samsa household, including Gregor, treats the metamorphosis in such a matter-of-fact way. "What should he do now?" Gregor wonders after waking up as a bug, realizing he's going to be late for work. "The next train went at seven; if he were to catch that he would have to rush like mad and the collection of samples was still not packed, and he did not at all feel particularly fresh and lively."

"He's in denial." This was Vincent's interpretation. "He wakes up in the morning and he's turned into a bug, but he's worrying about his alarm clock going off and not missing the train."

"Yes," I agreed. "When we can't grasp something enormous, we hold on to something small."

"When I was on trial," continued Vincent, "and I heard the judge say he was giving me two consecutive life sentences, all I could think about was the stuff in my bedroom at home—my posters, tapes, records, and everything—and what was going to happen to it. I couldn't register that I was about to go to prison for the rest of my life. You can't take it in, so you focus on something small. Everybody who comes to prison is in denial at first. You think it's all a big mistake. Somebody's going to find out what's happened, there'll be headlines in the newspaper, your attorney's going to get you out. It'll soon be over, and you'll be back home again. Then it finally sinks in. Nobody's going to rescue you. This is it. You're on your own."

Others were nodding their heads.

"It wasn't till after I'd been in prison for a year or so," continued Vincent, "that I woke up one day, looked around my cell, and I realized, 'I'm not a person anymore. I'm a parasite.'"

JULY 9, 2014

I'd been coming into the prison for almost two years now, but I was still making sense of the men's lives—how deprived they were—and hearing them express pleasure at seeing a photograph of my puppy or at the brightness of my summer clothing was a reminder of that deprivation. I got some insight into the daily indignities of their life in other, less pleasant ways, too, especially when I inadvertently did something to annoy a CO on whom I had to rely for various privileges. For the last few months I'd been permitted to walk through the compound and back without an escort, which made things immensely more convenient for me. Then, suddenly, everything changed. There was a CO I'd never seen before at the gate, a young African-American woman with an attitude. I'll call her Officer Grubb. She stopped me on the way to the school and told me I wasn't permitted to walk up without an escort.

"But I've been going up on my own for months," I argued.

"Well, that's against the rules," said Officer Grubb. The fact was, she was right. The other COs at the front gate had, happily for me, been turning a blind eye.

On this occasion I didn't have to wait long for an escort, and when I got to the classroom, only Donald and Turk were there. Since we had a little free time, I asked Turk if he'd show me the tattoo on his back. He stood up, glanced around furtively, turned around, and slipped off his shirt. The tattoo, smaller and far less dramatic than I'd imagined, was disappointing. Cursive script, indecipherable at first glance, covered the area around his left shoulder blade. From the way he'd described it, I'd pictured a huge crucifix taking up the whole of his back, like the tattoo Robert De Niro has in *Cape Fear*. Turk's wasn't a statement to the world, I realized, but a private memorial.

When I saw how personal his tattoo was, I felt suddenly ashamed. I'd had no right to ask Turk to take off his shirt. I was his teacher, not a prison guard. Nor was I his girlfriend, for that matter. I'd wanted to see his back tattoo ever since he'd described it to me—"I'll show it to you sometime," he'd said—and I couldn't imagine a better opportunity; but now it seemed not only risky (Turk would have been in real trouble if any of the COs had seen him without his shirt) but far too personal a request on my part, although Turk, to his credit, played it cool.

I quickly changed the subject.

"They wouldn't let me come up without an escort today," I told Donald while Turk was re-buttoning his shirt. "The CO was kind of nasty about it too."

"You must have pissed somebody off," he told me.

"Really?" I tried to imagine what I could have said or done.

"I'm still trying to work out who sent me up to Patuxent," said Donald. "I got a couple of ideas."

"Oh, yeah?"

"I'm starting to think it could be the assistant warden, right? I started to think back, see, and I recall having a little trouble some time ago with that particular lady. What happened is I got glaucoma, right? I cover up the windows in my cell. I got special permission from the warden, cause the daylight hurts my eyes. So one day the assistant warden sees my windows covered and wants to know whose cell it is. Somebody tells her it's my cell, and next thing I know, she wants to see me. I go to see her and I explain about my eyes, right? And she goes, 'No, you can't cover your windows, it's against the rules.' 'So,' I say to her, 'you're saying the rules are more important than my eyes?' She starts to reply, but I'm so pissed I'm already walking out of there, and as I leave, under my breath I go, 'Fuck the rules.' So now I'm thinking maybe she heard me, and sending me to Patuxent was her way of getting revenge."

If he was right, it was a petty and pointless act, but I was starting to see how paranoia could spread like the plague in a place like JCI, and how easy it was for the COs and the convicts to close ranks on one another. I could well believe a CO might take against a prisoner for some slight insult, imagined or otherwise, and look forward to the chance for revenge. I could see how the prison might function as a hothouse for seeds of irritation, which might easily grow into implacable hostilities.

One by one, the men filed in and sat down. J.D. was the last to arrive, followed by his new service dog, Hector. The animal's arrival elicited a spontaneous outburst of hooting and jeering from the men: Hector, it turned out, had just been neutered. He lay down, as usual, at the foot of his master's chair.

"Look at him. He looks embarrassed," laughed Turk, pointing at the dog.

"He's looking the other way," said Vincent. "He's so funny. Hey, Hector! Look, he won't meet your eyes!"

If Hector did look a little tender, I assumed he was sore from the operation, not embarrassed by the loss of his manhood.

"Knock it off, you guys." J.D was annoyed. "I'm sure he's feeling bad enough without all you idiots making him feel worse."

I began to ask questions about the second section of the text, but Kafka was no match for the freshly neutered Hector, and for the first time the men were almost unmanageable. While two or three of them may have been more interested in Gregor's metamorphosis than Hector's, it was difficult to keep a discussion going when every few minutes one of them would try to attract the dog's attention by hurling a pencil at him or cracking a joke about his posture or expression. I rarely got annoyed with the prisoners, but today I had a constant struggle to hide my frustration. Looking back, I wonder why I simply didn't tell them to stop being so childish.

"Childish" is the right word, and maybe that's why I didn't use it. Making fun of a freshly neutered dog is just the kind of thing little boys might do. Maybe I didn't stop them because I acknowledged, at an unconscious level, that for those infantilized by the prison system, there's some relief to be had in teasing a creature even more emasculated than they are.

The discussion we managed to have that day got tied up in the question of whether Gregor was still recognizable as Gregor. The men all imagined him as a sort of cockroach with a human face, like the semi-mutated scientist in *The Fly*. When we'd talked about other books, the men hadn't always been in agreement with me about the plot, but on this occasion it was nine against one—I assumed Gregor had no resemblance to his former self at all—and I couldn't help feeling a bit like Hector and wanting to cower under a chair. Since I could find nothing in the text that suggested either case—except the line "he found himself transformed into a giant insect," which to me seemed self-evident—the debate seemed pointless, and I kept trying to steer things in a different direction.

"If he were just a giant bug, not a Gregor bug, perhaps his situation would be even worse, because most people find insects so repulsive—especially cockroaches," I said. "Do you think that's because we associate them with dirt and disease, or is there some other reason? It's jolting, the way you come across them unexpectedly. I try not to kill spiders or flies, but I don't mind killing a cockroach."

"Me neither," agreed Vincent.

"Or getting somebody to kill it for me," I added, thinking about the enormous cockroach I'd recently encountered in the teachers' bathroom. I didn't want to use the toilet while it was crawling around on the floor, nor did I want to kill it. In the end I asked one of the prisoners if he'd mind going inside—the bathroom is unisex—and getting rid of it for me.

"Aw come on, Doc," he'd said. "You're not afraid of a little roach, are you?"

A little roach I could have handled, but this was not even a big roach. It was gargantuan.

"Me, I never kill a bug," announced Day-Day. "I might come back as one."

When we'd finished "The Black Cat," I'd given the men a copy of Poe's poem "The Raven" (many of them were big fans of the Baltimore Ravens, and I wanted to show them how the team came by its name). The prisoners had gotten into a discussion about what they'd do if a raven ever appeared in their cell. Vincent said he'd try to tame it and keep it as a pet. The men of the Noble Hearth regarded ravens as important symbols. But to Day-Day they were "nasty little fuckers."

"They peck out you eyes," he'd informed us. "I'd kill that nasty little motherfucker before it killed me."

Since he clearly wouldn't think twice about killing a raven, I wondered why Day-Day was so worried about the possibility of cosmic payback for murdering a roach. Things fell into place when I read his written work and remembered that Day-Day himself was the adopted child of violently abusive parents. Clearly he felt a special connection to Gregor:

> This story I like it a lot because this can happen to anybody but in another situation. Like for instance I was like a Gregor. I woke up one day and look back when I was a happy child for a few seconds then the loud noises at the door Day-Day open the door. Next like Gregor the abuse started pushed and shoved down the hallway hitting wall after wall to the basement door. Then pushed down steps in the dark door slammed. I just wanted to be accepted for who I was like Gregor. We are no different.

"I think Gregor's always been a sort of Gregor bug," said Sig. "Like a worker ant, you know, working for the collective. He's got no individuality. Maybe he did at one time, but it's been squashed."

"What's the collective in this case?" I asked. "The workforce?"

"Could be. Or it could be the family," said Sig.

"It could just be society," added Steven. "Everybody doing the same thing, going to work, coming home, having dinner."

"Same thing as goes on here," Sig went on. "Prisoners—you might as well say insects—all dressed in blue, one big swarm, all swarming through the yard or into the chow hall. We all look the same from the outside. That's part of the point, I guess. We're not individuals anymore. We're just numbers and uniforms."

Even the COs were constantly transferred from tier to tier—a rule enforced so they never got close to the prisoners, and learned instead to see them as abstractions rather than individuals.

"So you're saying Gregor's a criminal?" asked Nick, who tended to take things literally.

"Well, the guy, the what's-his-name—the Chief Clerk— thinks he is," said Sig. "He thinks he's stolen those cash deposits."

We looked up the passage Sig had mentioned, since none of us had any memory of it. The Chief Clerk, addressing Gregor through the closed door of his room, says, "Your employer did suggest a possible reason for your failure to appear . . . it had to do with the money that was recently entrusted to you."

"Maybe that be why everybody want to get in his room," suggested Day-Day, hitching up his pants. "They all think he done got that bread in there, man. They all, like, come on man, open the door."

"So he's not a criminal but he's suspected of being one," I said. "The Chief Clerk doesn't trust him. I was wondering if any of you guys could identify with him."

"Not me," said Turk, shaking his head. "I can't imagine going to sleep and waking up a big ugly-ass bug. I'd rather die in my sleep!"

"I can imagine what it would be like to wake up and be somebody different, to change overnight," said Nick. "I mean, that's happened to all of us. We may not have changed physically, but we've woken up in the morning as murderers, rapists, whatever. Totally different creatures."

"I was thinking about it. It would be pretty bad. If I had to be an insect, I'd rather wake as a butterfly or a ladybird, something that's not so ugly," said Donald.

"What bothered me was the rejection from his parents," said J.D. "Whatever had happened to him, basically he was sick. He had no control over it. And they wouldn't accept the fact that he was sick. It's like parents whose kids have mental illness, and they're embarrassed by them and lock them away somewhere."

"I was trying to identify with him," said Steven. "I thought a lot about how it would feel to be a bug. I think I'd miss my hands the most. Having tiny spindly legs would be bad enough. Trying to use your mouth in place of fingers would be pretty hard."

When I left the prison school that day, the CO at the door let me out as usual, with no escort. As I walked down the hall and through the door to the compound, however, I heard somebody hammering, and when I turned around, I saw the guard in the glass box overlooking the sally port beating on the glass to get my attention. She shouted that I had to go back and wait for an escort. I turned back and, running into a male CO who was on his way out, asked if he'd escort me to the front gate. He did. When I reached the metal detector, however, Officer Grubb began reprimanding me angrily.

"*Did you hear what I said?*" she yelled. "*You need an escort both ways! Both coming out and going back!*"

"But I had an escort," I objected.

Officer Grubb leaned into my face.

"*Are you listening to me?*" she shouted. "*I know you try to leave on your own. They called me on the radio to tell me. You better listen to me in the future or you'll be in big trouble!*"

I walked through the parking lot to my car, feeling shaken up. For just a moment the unaccustomed sensation of mounting tears pricked the backs of my eyes. I felt like a child who'd been suddenly and unexpectedly chastised. It was a primitive, humiliating emotion, one I hadn't felt for many years.

JULY 16, 2014

Until now, I'd been careful not to make waves at JCI. As a woman in a men's prison, this wasn't easy; but so far I had a clean slate, a low profile, and—as far as I knew—no enemies.

The following week, as soon as I arrived, I knew everything had changed. The CO at the gate was waiting for me. She knew my name. It wasn't Officer Grubb this time but the light-skinned CO who'd called me out of the classroom to tell me that the men were trying to peek up my skirt. I didn't know her name but she knew mine. As soon as I stepped through the gate, she looked me up and down—I got the feeling she was deciding what to find fault with—then said very firmly, "Ms. Brottman, you can't come in here in that dress."

It was a floor-length maxidress.

"Is there a problem with it?" I asked her.

"It's see-through."

"But I'm wearing a slip," I protested.

"Let me see. Come here. Stand in the light."

If she couldn't tell, I thought, how would anyone else notice? Nonetheless, I walked into the light as instructed and the CO lifted up the hem and inspected my petticoat like a Victorian schoolmistress.

"Your slip doesn't come down far enough" was her verdict.

I knew there was no point arguing: her objection had nothing to do with my maxidress. She wanted to remind me of my place. I walked back to my car and drove once again to the nearby thrift store. I grabbed the first floor-length skirt I saw and stood in line at the counter to pay. Back in the front seat of my car, I struggled to pull on the new skirt under my dress.

"Are you teaching *The Purpose Driven Life?*" asked my escort when I was finally let into the prison. She must have thought that anybody who wore three layers of skirts in the heat of July had to be pretty damned "purpose-driven."

For that day's session I'd asked the men to put themselves in the role of Gregor's sister, Grete, and write a letter to a close friend explaining what's happening to her brother. The men seemed to thrive on exercises like this. They seemed to love getting outside their own heads for a while. Some of them— Steven, Sig, and Nick in particular—would enter the spirit of the story, matching their own style and vocabulary to that of the narrator's. Steven's letter began, "Dear brother Gregor has fallen into a rare and unexplainable illness." Donald did the same, but with a humorous twist: "*Guten Tag*, Ava. Remember how you used to say my brother was creepy? Well, you're not going to believe this, but now not only is he creepy, he's also a crawler." Day-Day, on the other hand, took the story, dragged it out of Kafka's world, and brought it into his own. This was one of the things that drew me to him. He seemed to live in a perpetual present. He had no sense of history, cultures, or times other than his own. "Dear Tee-Tee," he wrote. "My brother is a bug. Girl stop laughing I no you are but its true and the whole house is going crazy. I sent you a picture of him to your phone did you get it? secret secret secret."

Each of the prisoners had very different versions of Grete, many of them based on their own sisters, and after talking about Grete, we began to discuss Gregor's relationship with his family.

"It really makes you wonder why anyone would choose to be a parent," I said, half jokingly. "Don't even the cutest kids become teenagers—unrecognizable creatures who lock themselves in their rooms, just like Gregor?"

The prisoners had heard my views on this subject before. Some of them thought I was cold and hardhearted because I didn't have children and didn't want any, though I doted on my pets. I, on the other hand, liked to make fun of the prisoners' sentimental clichés about happy families—clichés they really seemed to believe, despite all evidence to the contrary (although it's admittedly difficult to be a hands-on dad when you're serving a life sentence in prison).

We may have disagreed on the question of the family, but we did agree, in the end, that Gregor's strange and rather cruel family was better off without him, and that *The Metamorphosis* raised essential questions not only about the nature of relationships but also about what makes us human. At the very end of the discussion, I compared Gregor's state of mind as a cockroach to that of some of the heavily medicated patients in the psychiatric hospital where I also volunteered.

"I was talking to a guy there last week," I told them, "and he said he was perfectly rational when he came in. They put him on a huge dose of Stelazine, and he said it turned him into a vegetable. The next thing he knew, it was eight years later."

"Stelazine," said Donald, pretending to write it down. "How do you spell it? I gotta get myself some of that stuff."

10

LOLITA

We finished *The Metamorphosis* in summer 2014. In the fall, I carried on visiting the prison every week, but not for the book club, from which I took a break for a while. As an experiment, I taught a writing class to a mixed group of prisoners and college students. All the men in the book club were enrolled, so I continued to see them regularly, although they were part of a much larger group. Once we got past security, this class was always interesting, but the weekly stress of getting fifteen creatively dressed and plentifully pierced art students past Officer Grubb and through the metal detector caused such damage to my nerves that I don't plan to repeat the experiment anytime soon.

As the semester came to an end, something unexpected happened; at least, I wasn't expecting it. The prisoners often told me that their lawyers were renegotiating their sentences, that they'd be getting a new court date at any time now, that next summer they'd be lying on the beach, and so on. Nothing ever came of these predictions, so when Vincent told me he'd be out in November, I didn't pay much attention. After all, he'd served only a little over thirty years, and however long that might seem, it wasn't anywhere near the two consecutive life sentences the judge had given him. But what I didn't know was his lawyer was Howard Cardin, brother of the United States senator for Maryland Ben Cardin, and an attorney with a reputation for performing miracles. (He was Known at JCI as "Go Home" Cardin.) What's more, Cardin and his team were representing Vincent pro bono, since Cardin was an old friend of Vincent's father. I was not aware that Cardin had managed to get Vincent's original two sentences commuted into one, so I was taken by surprise when I returned to the prison in November and learned that Vincent had been released.

Doug, a stately gentleman of sixty-six (and another titan at six feet five inches), took Vincent's place in the book club. Doug had just got out of the hospital. He'd been suffering from an aortic aneurysm that had caused a leaky heart valve and was on a lot of new medication that was making him very groggy.

As a matter of fact, I'd heard of Doug before I started working in the prison. His was a notorious case in Baltimore history. I live in an old hotel called the Belvedere, and while researching the history of the building I'd come across newspaper accounts of the "Belvedere trunk murder," a crime that took place in May 1973, when Doug and his coworker Dennis had been managing the then-vacant hotel. Doug was convicted of murdering a local man and concealing his body in a trunk on the basis of testimony from Dennis, with whom the victim was last seen alive. Doug was single-mindedly determined to clear his name. He constantly wrote to local newspapers about his own situation and

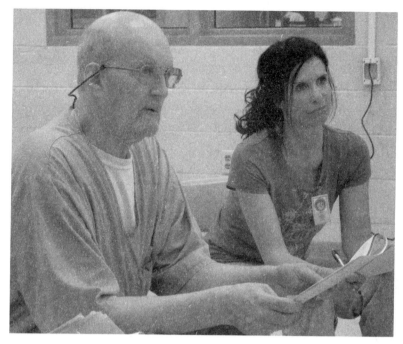

DOUG AND MIKITA

related legal matters, communicated with various lawyers, and campaigned for reporters to revisit his case. His medical problems had caused a setback in his crusade, but he continued to insist he'd be exonerated before he died. When I first met him, he was awaiting a hearing on newly discovered—and potentially exculpatory—evidence.

At JCI, a new money-saving policy had been introduced. Now, every Wednesday, the prison was on "administrative lockdown." After breakfast, no one was let out of their cells except those men with essential jobs, including those who worked in Dietary. The kitchen workers would prepare lunch and dinner trays, and at mealtimes the prisoners would walk over to the dining hall, pick up a tray, and take it back to their cells. All Wednesday visits, appointments, and meetings were canceled. Fortunately, the warden allowed classes to continue even on lockdown days. Since these weekly lockdowns had been saving the prison a significant amount of money, it looked as though they'd continue indefinitely.

FEBRUARY 26, 2015

Back at JCI, I was pleased to see my old friends again and happy to meet a new one: Luke, J.D.'s new six-month-old black Labrador, who was still partly floppy puppy. J.D. himself was also uncharacteristically floppy. He'd broken his hand playing handball and was taking Percocet to numb the pain. It was, he announced in an unexpectedly loud voice, the first time he'd ever taken a narcotic of any kind. His eyes were wide and he was slumped halfway down in his chair.

"Percocet's nothing," said Donald, whose two herniated disks had made him long familiar with both pain and pain medication. Today he made a grand entrance, walking stiffly with the help of a cane. "They've got me on methadone now."

"Is that all they can do for you, just give you drugs to numb the pain?" I asked.

"They've tried physical therapy. Now they're trying pain management. In the end, when they've been through everything else, they're going to have to operate."

"How do you manage to work in the woodshop if you're in so much pain?"

"It's all computerized. I can sit down. Just got to press the right buttons."

Turk had some news for me. "We've had an interesting event the other day," he told me. "You probably saw it on the news. This guy got steamed to death."

"*Steamed* to death?"

"That's right. I'll tell you how it happened. His wife, on the outside, she got killed. This guy, he had a breakdown, so they put him on mental health segregation, so called. Stripped him down. You know how cold it's been this winter, right? It was, like, minus two, three degrees? What I heard was he was asking for a blanket, and they wouldn't give him one. They think he pulled the top pipe out of the radiator, maybe to get warm, maybe to kill himself, they don't know. The janitor saw water coming out from under the cell, and he looked in the door and sees this guy on the floor. Anyway, by the time the police got there, the guy was dead."

"God, how awful."

"Yeah. He was a real light-complected guy. When they found him, his skin had gone pink. They said it slid right off his body just like soft-shell shrimp."

"No kidding."

"That's what they said," confirmed Donald.

There was a long pause.

"So, what else is going on?" I asked. "Are you guys taking any courses?"

"I'm taking two," said Steven. "Criminal Justice and Shakespeare."

"Shakespeare?"

"Yeah. We've really been having a lot of fun with it." Steven gave me his brightest, most wicked grin. "We're reading *Romeo and Juliet* and we've been acting it all out."

"Seriously? Are you reading it in the original or in modern English?"

"The original."

"And you're enjoying it?"

"Oh, yeah," he laughed. "At first a lot of the guys didn't want to play women's parts. Then the professor laid down the law. She goes, 'Look, in Shakespeare's time, no ladies were allowed on the stage. It was all men. Boys had to play the ladies' parts. You're going to have to do the same thing here, so you may as well all get over your shyness right now.' Donald had gone to the bathroom, and when he came back he found out he was my wife."

Everyone started to laugh as Steven recalled how Donald found himself in the role of "Mrs. Capulet," but I was more concerned about the discomfort in my stomach. Was it something I ate? No. I recognized it, although at first I couldn't tell what it was. It was something I hadn't felt for a long time. Then I knew: jealousy. I was jealous! "My" men were reading Shakespeare with another teacher. Another female teacher! Not only that, they were reading the text in the original, acting it out, and enjoying it. Shakespeare was *my* territory! The jealousy lasted for around thirty seconds, at which point it was replaced with a different emotion, equally painful: dismay that I was still capable of such petty resentments. Fortunately, by the time Steven had finished his anecdote, I'd recovered my equilibrium and was back on an even keel.

At least, I thought, no one else but me would dare ask the men to read *Lolita*, although I still wasn't sure it was a good idea. I'd changed my mind about it many times. *Lolita* was a book I loved, but I knew it would be controversial, and I wasn't even sure if the CO at the gate would let me bring copies into the prison, especially since the cover of the edition I'd chosen was illustrated by a pair of coltish legs emerging from a schoolgirl's skirt. I needn't have worried. The guard scarcely gave it a glance, and when I handed out copies to the men, Steven mentioned there was a copy in the "Classics" section of the prison library. That was a huge relief.

The men were all familiar with "Lolita" as a slang term for a sexually precocious young girl, although they didn't necessarily realize that when the book was first published in 1955, the pedophile wasn't the familiar demon he's become today. I'm sure Nabokov would have been shocked to learn that pedophilia would come to be so universally despised that in some places sentences for child rape can be more severe than those for murder (which, some have argued, may encourage such rapists to kill their victims, destroying all evidence of the "more serious" crime).

I first read *Lolita* in 1989. I spent that summer almost broke, sleeping on the floor of a friend's dorm room and washing dishes for cash. I saw a copy in a local bookstore—the 1980 British Penguin edition—and was drawn in by the cover. Beneath an alluring quote ("The greatest novel of rapture in modern fiction") a young girl wearing red heart-shaped sunglasses sucked a red lollipop—an homage to the Kubrick film, I now realize, as Nabokov's Lolita does neither. As soon as I started reading, I knew I was in the hands of a genius. I was mesmerized. The effect, I later realized, was intentional. Just as Poe meant his tales to evoke the uncanny effect of a séance, Nabokov wanted to cast a spell over his readers. The writer, he declared, had to be "at once a storyteller, a teacher, and, most supremely, an enchanter."

There was no enchantment in the air, however, the day we began reading *Lolita* at JCI. The sky outside was gray, and water dripped from the gutter above the classroom onto the compound outside. Maybe it was the miserable weather, but the men seemed apathetic. There was no spark. Everything felt choppy and fractured. Day-Day had to leave early to go to a group called Men of Character. J.D. was too medicated to focus. Donald had forgotten his reading glasses again. At first I thought it was Vincent's absence that was making things feel off balance. Then I wondered whether the break I'd taken had been too long. Then I noticed something else: the men weren't sitting in their usual places. The seat they'd saved for me today wasn't between Charles and Steven, as it had always been until now, but between Nick and Donald. Steven was sitting directly opposite me, on the other side of the room, in between J.D. and Sig. I'm not sure this change of formation was a cause of the difference, or a symptom of it, but it definitely made me feel ill at ease.

Later I wondered whether the slump could be attributed to the fact that, right from the start, the men seemed suspicious of the narrator. About an hour into our session, after reading aloud a description of Humbert Humbert sitting on a park bench under which a little girl is groping for a lost marble, Sig looked up at me with an expression of utter disgust and exclaimed, "This guy's just an old pedo!"

When I'd imagined reading *Lolita* with the prisoners—many of whom had committed crimes that might be considered as serious as child rape—I'd thoughtlessly assumed they'd have sympathy for Humbert Humbert as well as for Lolita. I thought they'd see him as a fellow outsider. I'd always believed that anyone who engages fully with *Lolita* has to understand that a story of what is technically termed "sexual molestation" can also be a deeply moving love story. There's no "for or against" in *Lolita*; it's a portrait of two suffering human beings.

After our first session on *Lolita*, I saw what I should have seen months ago: that, rather than sympathizing with Humbert Humbert, the men would despise him. I'd learned from reading *Junkie* that the prisoners wouldn't necessarily recognize their fictional counterparts, nor did I always expect them to identify with the lawbreaker. In the case of *Lolita*, however, I'd never considered

Humbert to be anything other than an idol. I've always had a weakness for eloquent gentleman, and when I first read *Lolita*, I immediately fell in love with the narrator. Whenever I read the book, Humbert Humbert's style, humor, and sophistication blind me to his faults. I know that, in prison, pedophiles are considered despicable scum—it was just that I'd never thought of Humbert as a pedophile. And now, poor Humbert—I'd thrown him to a lynch mob. As I drove back to Baltimore, I wondered if the men would refuse to go on reading the book. It hadn't happened yet, but if they were going to veto any of my choices, this would be the one. The prisoners had a far more passionate sense of justice than I did. The outcast is always looking for someone to throw rocks at.

I've always felt immense sympathy for Humbert Humbert. I believe he's acutely conscious of his failings and painfully aware of the misery he's caused. He's always known that his passion is hopeless, that Lolita has never loved him at all, that she's not old enough to love him. Worse, he knows precisely what he's done to her. "Something within her [had] been broken by me," he confesses, an acknowledgment that's reinforced in the novel's final scene. Standing on a ridge above a small town in Colorado, he hears the faint, distant sounds of children playing and knows that "the hopelessly poignant thing was not Lolita's absence from my side, but the absence of her voice from that concord." If he were his own judge, Humbert tells us, he'd give himself "thirty-five years for rape." Of course, these passages came much later on in the book. The prisoners hadn't read them yet. Perhaps they never would.

When I got home that afternoon, I looked up information about the man who was steamed to death. It was just as Turk had said. The prisoner, who was serving a thirty-year sentence for murdering his girlfriend in 2008, was "found unresponsive . . .

inside his cell, which was full of steam." It was unclear whether his death was an accident or a suicide. A review of the incident was being conducted, and three correctional officers had been placed on "routine administrative leave."

MARCH 11, 2015

Heavy snow had kept the prison school closed for two weeks; today it finally felt a little closer to spring. As I drove past the freight train cutting opposite the prison, I noticed crows had started building their nests in the still-bare trees.

The mood of the group felt slightly better today, although the men kept to their new seating arrangement, and it took a while for things to settle down, as there was a lot of noise in the hall. It might have been coming from the chapel, which was right next to our classroom, but it sounded less like preaching or praying than an angry, ongoing argument. Finally, at my request, Day-Day got up and closed the door as far as he could without locking it. Although it was warmer than the last time we'd met, there was still a chill in the air, and most of the men were wearing long-sleeved shirts layered under their T-shirts. Nick alone was wearing baggy shorts and his old, faithful "Coma Cola" T-shirt, so threadbare that it was almost an abstraction. I tried to imagine the expression on Officer Grubb's face if I'd tried coming into the prison clad in something so notional.

We'd missed two weeks of classes, but the men had kept up with their reading and by now were halfway through the book. I was pleased they'd continued with *Lolita*, although they still despised Humbert Humbert. J.D. was especially outspoken, and I wondered whether this was because Vincent was no longer in the group to overshadow him. His broken hand was encased in a huge cast, with only his thumb visible, and when it came to Humbert Humbert, it pointed straight down.

"It really bothers me when he uses all the French," he began. "None of us can understand it. It seems like he just wants to show you how superior he is."

Everyone nodded.

"Unfortunately, French lessons aren't on offer in this particular facility," Sig added.

"You won't find too many cosmopolitans in here," Doug agreed. "Nor will you find many 'metrosexuals,' as people call them today."

"But it's not just the French," J.D. went on. "It's all bullshit, all his long, fancy words. I can see through it. It's all a cover-up. I know what he wants to do to her."

This annoyed me. "You can't simply dismiss the language as though it's irrelevant, like a veil disguising something horrible. Take away the language and there's no *Lolita*."

"I know what J.D.'s saying, though." Steven joined the debate. "Like, that thing with Annabel Leigh. It's like he's looking back and trying to pretty it all up. It just made me think he must have had something to hide."

Charles agreed. "Humbert sounds very persuasive, but we've only got his side of things. I feel like he's making excuses for his behavior. Bottom line, he's trying to cover up the fact that he's a pedophile."

Now I was even more irritated. "There is no 'bottom line,'" I said. "This is a love story."

Charles, sitting to my right, muttered, "That's a crock right there."

"What's a crock?"

"What you just said," he sneered. "This isn't a *love story*. Get rid of all the fancy language, bring it down to the lowest common denominator, and it's a grown man molesting a little girl is what it is."

"But you can't do that!" I was outraged. "This isn't a court case where we're trying to work out what happened. We can't throw out everything that doesn't matter. It *all* matters! This is literature!"

Charles sighed, sat back, and stretched out his legs. I knew he was about to launch into one of his long analogies. No interruptions would be permitted.

"You know," he began, "this shrink told me that I could walk into a beautiful, freshly painted room, and if the painters had missed one single spot, I'd find it right away. No matter what color or how beautiful the paint is, no matter how clever, skillful, or talented the painters are, no matter what stroke or style is used, this spot can't be covered up. Well, in this story, the spot on the wall is pedophilia."

"I completely disagree with you," I said.

"I kind of thought you might," he replied.

One of my initial hesitations about reading *Lolita* in the book club was my concern that Nabokov's style would be too difficult for the men. Now I realized it wasn't nearly as convoluted as Conrad's, although Nabokov used more foreign phrases and literary allusions. The problem was that I saw language as central to *Lolita*, but the prisoners saw it as a way to make the vile lusts of a pedophile seem high-minded, a smoke screen to distract gullible intellectuals who fell for a fancy prose style. In other words, fools like me.

I wasn't the only one who liked the book. Others were enjoying it, too, but not for the same reasons. Day-Day, dressed in an orange knit skullcap and wearing orange-tinted sunglasses, told us that he liked the book because he loved Lolita. He'd reached the part where she was starting to charge Humbert for the sexual favors she once gave him for free.

"Lolita getting smart," he said. "When I read this part, I thought, 'Damn, my Lolita growing up.' She take control, playing the pimp, She doing bad things at school. She know Humbert do everything she want him to do."

He then left for his Men of Character group.

"Any other opinions?"

"To be honest, this book is boring the crap out of me," said Nick. "They're just driving around. Nothing's happening anymore. We don't need all this description. We know what the countryside looks like."

I wish I could have helped these men, stuck in their six-by-seven-foot prison cells, to find more satisfaction in Nabokov's glorious descriptions of the American landscape. In my own case, after eighteen years in the U.S., the magic of the countryside remains for me: in fireflies, watermelon, whirring cicadas, hummingbirds, and summer thunderstorms. I'm still entranced, like Humbert Humbert, by the ever-changing landscape: cliffs, groves, pine forests, sage brush, "blueberry woods," "red bluffs ink-blotted with junipers," "heart and sky-piercing snow-veined gray colossi of stone." Given these congenial descriptions, I was surprised to learn that many of the book's early readers—especially the British and French—found *Lolita* to be resolutely "anti-American." Nabokov denied the charge, pronouncing the novel's tender landscape details—the red barns and green corn—as his tribute paid to this "lovely, trustful, dreamy, enormous country."

MARCH 18, 2015

I'd never thought of *Lolita* as a story about pedophilia. To me, it was a love story and a story about language. I'd always considered language, as much as Lolita, to be Humbert's tragic, tormented passion. He loves to describe her skin, her clothes, her voice, her "frail, honey-hued shoulders," her "silky supple bare back," her "chestnut head of hair," her ears, her toes, the light hair on her arms and legs. She's a word as well as a body. Just seeing her name in a class list gives Humbert such a "spine-thrill of delight" that he's moved to tears—"hot, opalescent, thick tears that poets and lovers shed." Ironically, it's the very person making her suffer who evokes the reader's compassion for Lolita. It's this surface disjunction, for me at least, that provides *Lolita* with its magical, heart-rending tension. There's another level of tension, too, between Humbert's pain and his language. Charlotte is intoxicated by the way he speaks; she finds it artful and elegant, but to Lolita—and the men in the book club—it's an embarrassment and a lie.

It bothered me that the prisoners seemed unable to separate Nabokov from Humbert Humbert. They couldn't believe that the person writing about Humbert's sexual interests didn't share those sexual interests himself. When I talked about the imagination, and research, and Nabokov's long and healthy marriage, they seemed suspicious. I found it difficult to understand why they couldn't separate the two, why they were so angered by Humbert Humbert's "fancy words," and why they found it so difficult to trust him. If his voice had no consistency or plausibility, after all, we'd be unable to engage with the story in any way. He may be deranged, dodgy, or deluded, but he's still describing what he believes to be true. You could make the case that most of the time Humbert tells the story in such a way as to justify his own behavior, but isn't this how we all tell our stories, consciously or not?

I believe Humbert is honest about his feelings. In other circumstances—when he's describing the American landscape, or the town of Ramsdale, or Lolita's body—he's given us no reason not to trust him, bearing in mind he's writing a retrospective account of his life for the benefit of judge and jury. If he elicits our sympathy, it's because he observes so much and because his descriptions are so striking and original, not because he skews them to his advantage; he does not. As a matter of fact, he's intensely clear-eyed and self-critical, always reminding us of his biases and exaggerations. It's impossible for the sensitive reader not to realize, for example, that Charlotte is far more intelligent and complex than the clownish caricature Humbert presents us with. And although he loves Lolita obsessively, he readily admits she can be "a most exasperating brat."

Yet the men were unable to let go of the pedophile question. To me, *that* was exasperating. They never seemed to want to talk about anything else. They seemed to be blind to everything that I loved about the book.

"Can't we manage to have a discussion of Lolita without using the word 'pedophile'?" I asked them. "Why can't we ever get away from that word?"

"I'll tell you why," said Turk. "Because a lot of guys in here, their sisters or girlfriends or their cousins have had their lives ruined by guys like this Mr. Humbert Humbert. Me personally, I've found this book very difficult to read for that reason. I got three daughters, and there's a lot of family issues it brings up."

"Turk's right," agreed Sig. "When I was first locked up, my daughters were aged five and six. For a long time, I really worried about them meeting somebody like Humbert Humbert and me being stuck here in prison and not being able to do anything about it. It really bothered me." I remembered pictures Sig had shown me of his daughters when they were younger: beautiful, long-limbed girls, one blonde and one brunette, with Sig's eyes and mouth. These days, I gathered, they were no longer in close contact with their father. I could see why reading a book like *Lolita* might upset him.

"It's a sensitive topic," said Donald thoughtfully. "This is some of the most believable fiction I've ever read. And one of the reasons it's so sensitive is that here in this prison there's a whole lot of Humbert Humberts. Matter of fact, we're surrounded by them."

"I understand it's a sensitive topic," I said. "But one of the things *Lolita* has taught me is that everybody is unique. There's no such thing as 'just an old pedo' like Sig said. Even if you find somebody's behavior reprehensible, pedophiles are people like you and me, individuals with histories, backgrounds, families, and relationships. I disagree that Humbert's only interested in sex. Sex always spills over into other kinds of experiences and emotions, like the need to be loved, or to express power, or to leave your mark. Remember, Lolita had a huge crush on Humbert at first. And she'd had sex before. If he exploits her, she also exploits him, to a degree. It's complicated, like all relationships."

There was a long pause. Finally, Doug broke the silence.

"Any of you guys remember Ellwood Leuschner over in Baltimore Penitentiary?" he asked. Doug had served time in a number of different prisons.

A couple of the older guys nodded.

"This guy Ellwood Leuschner was just like Humbert Humbert," explained Doug. "He was real smart. Had an amazing vocabulary.

Matter of fact, he had a reputation for being a wonderful jailhouse lawyer because he was so intelligent. He actually got a lot of men out. Now, this guy was a pedophile. He'd raped and killed some young children in Salisbury, up there by the Campbell's soup factory. Horrible crimes. I'd avoided him the whole time I was at the penitentiary, because that's just the way it works with pedophiles. You keep away from them. But this guy was so smart, I was curious. Anyway, one day I saw him on his own—he was in the gym—so I took my chance. I went up and I said to him, 'Leuschner, can I ask you something?' And he said to me, 'Doug, I know what you're going to ask. And I've gotta tell you, I've thought about it for years and years, and I've spent my whole life trying to figure it out and make sense of it. And all I can tell you is this. Something comes over me, and I can't control myself. And that's all I know.'"

MARCH 26, 2015

There'd been an outbreak of norovirus at JCI. The men were in a good mood when we met, and the atmosphere was lively. They wanted to tell me all about the bug that had been going around, who'd caught it, and what their symptoms had been. They didn't seem to want to talk about *Lolita*. Steven especially was even more upbeat than usual. He'd just received news that his mentor, who'd offered to share his home with Steven upon his release, had also hired him a prestigious attorney—in fact, none other than "Go Home" Cardin. Apparently, Cardin thought that if things went well, Steven could be out of prison by August. A year ago I'd have seen this as wishful thinking, but after Vincent's release, I'd seen for myself what could happen. (In fact, Steven was released on June 24.)

The men were supposed to have finished *Lolita* by this week, and I had to interrupt the conversation to ask for their final verdicts.

Turk wiped his brow theatrically. "Man!" he said. "I thought that other cat was hard!"

"Shakespeare?" I asked.

"No, not Shakespeare, that other cat."

"Poe?"

"Yeah, that's it, Poe. Edgar Allan Poe."

"This guy can really write, though," said Donald. "You can fall in love with the story even though you hate what it's about, because you like the language so much. It draws you in. You almost start to get misled."

"What do you mean, 'get misled'?" I asked him.

"You almost start to feel sorry for the guy."

"Why shouldn't you feel sorry for him?" I asked. "Isn't he suffering?"

There was an uncomfortable pause. Then Doug spoke.

"In here," he said, "we're all used to listening to police and prosecutors. They see everything we say as ways of rationalizing the seriousness of the charges against us. They think that whatever we say is said to mislead other people. And I guess we've sort of internalized their way of looking at things, because to us, Humbert's highfalutin language is a kind of ruse. Instead of being impressed by it, we automatically wonder what he's trying to hide."

"That's a good point," said Sig. "Like, I noticed there's not one single curse word in the entire book so far, and I thought, 'What's wrong with this guy? What's he trying to hide? Why can't he just tell it like it is?'"

"Still," Steven concurred. "You've got to admire him. Whatever you say about him, he's slick as shit at what he does. If he were a forger, he'd be the world's best forger. If he were a cat burglar, he'd be the world's best cat burglar. It turns out that he's a pedophile, and you could say he's king of the pedophiles."

"You know, I'm starting to get interested in the guy," said Charles.

"Really?" I was surprised. "After everything you've said?"

He nodded. "I've let go of the spot on the wall. I've managed to get over the fact that this book is all about a slick-talking pervert."

"How did you do that?"

"I don't know. It just happened. I just found myself getting more involved in the story. Humbert was starting to get reckless and stupid. I just knew he was going to get caught. Our tier was on lockdown all day Tuesday, so I finished it then."

"Oh?"

"Yeah. On Monday night a guy got stabbed. It was around 9:30, which is when they lock us in for the evening. I was in my cell, so I didn't see what happened, but I saw them carrying the guy who'd been stabbed off the tier."

"So, thanks to the guy getting stabbed, you developed an interest in *Lolita*."

"I guess you could say that."

"Charlie's right. You want to know what happens," Sig explained. "That's what's held my interest. I wanted Humbert to get what's coming to him."

"It should have happened a long time ago," said Turk. "Where's that Poe when you really need him?"

"But you don't like Poe," I said.

Turk laughed. "I said, 'Where's the Po-Po when you really need them? I'm talking about the po-lice. They should have arrested this Mr. Humbert a long time ago. But he's too smart for them. He was a player. A smooth operator."

"I'm glad Lolita got away, but she should have escaped a lot earlier," said Steven.

"Remember, he basically told her that if she ever tried turning him in, they'd arrest him and put her in an orphanage?" Donald reminded him. "That was smart, because she believed him. She thought being with Humbert would be better than what would happen to her if she was on her own."

"Right. He said he was trying to protect her, but he was actually trying to hide her from the law," said Steven. "It made things worse for her in the end. That guy Quilty was another pedo."

I got stuck in traffic on the way back to Baltimore that afternoon—there'd been an accident on the highway—and as I sat in my car waiting for things to start moving again, I had to face the fact that, much to my dismay, the prisoners had got it right. These men, some of whom were guilty of terrible crimes, had immediately sympathized with twelve-year-old Lolita. They recognized at once that she was suffering. They talked about her mother's cruelty, her sobs in the night, her loneliness, her entrapment, her abuse by Humbert Humbert and later by Quilty. And I, with my weakness for a fancy prose style, had fallen into Nabokov's trap and could see Lolita only through Humbert's eyes, as his invention, his nymphet. I could not make sense of or see her, as the prisoners did, as a little girl in her own right. Instead, I believed what Humbert told me. I was taken in by him. I thought he was a special case. I wanted to analyze the narrator and his prose, to reach deeper and further layers and levels of psychological complexity, to scrutinize and dissect his sentence structure and word choice; but all the time this was leading me further and further away from the main fact of the matter: Lolita's pain.

APRIL 9, 2015

For our last session on *Lolita*, we sat down to watch the Stanley Kubrick movie adaptation from 1962, which I've always loved, mostly because of James Mason's performance as Humbert Humbert. After the experience with *Macbeth*, I was a little worried the prisoners might find it boring, as it's shot in black-and-white and there are no explicit sex or action scenes. But this time the men managed to stay awake. It was hot in the classroom, yet despite the heat I felt profoundly comfortable, with a large fan blowing behind me and Luke snoring quietly on the floor to my left. The men were slumped in their seats chewing candy, sharing private jokes and comments, and chuckling to themselves quietly (or not so quietly, in Doug's case). I liked being in the hot room with the men; I enjoyed their lazy, accepting camaraderie.

As I was driving home, however, I started to rethink this notion of camaraderie. How genuine was it? Sometimes it seemed like an illusion. Were the prisoners really allies, or was it just a temporary bonding? Most of them were no doubt very lonely at times, but were they any lonelier than people on the outside? Then I remembered how surprised I was when, after the book club had been meeting for more than two years, one of the men, in conversation, referred to "that really tall guy," meaning Nick. Even now, after almost three years, I know for a fact there were men in the book club who didn't know the names of other men in the group. When I wondered how this could be—there were only nine of them, and I addressed them by name all the time—I realized it didn't mean they weren't aware of one another. It just meant they'd learned to mind their own business and act as if they didn't know, even if they did.

Some of the prisoners, I felt, seemed bound together insepa-rably. A few had known one another for decades, and between them I'd seen expressions of what appeared to be deep affection and respect. But when I pointed this out, Charles was quick to reply. "Yeah, I'm sure you've seen that," he said, in his usual tone of half-repressed belligerence. "But what you haven't seen is the anger, frustration, misery, hate, suffering, and other things like violence and death. The depth of pain and mental and emotional conflict that we endure is something we can escape from for an hour or so in this group, and that's why you've never seen it."

I've never seen it, but that doesn't mean I'm incapable of imag-ining it. The longer I continued with the book club, the more I thought about the men when I was away from them. I thought about their sadness and their pain. I also thought about how spe-cial solidarities can extend through a physically closed-off place, how isolated people come to rely on one another for assistance and emotional support, like the proverbial community of strang-ers that comes together in the face of a catastrophe. No doubt those who were released would disappear into their respective communities and never see one another again, but those who foresaw no chance of release knew that, like it or not, they'd spend the rest of their lives together.

I was lucky. I wasn't caught up in the catastrophe. Each week, after my time at the prison was over, I was free to go. But I grew so fond of these nine men, and I got so much pleasure from their company, that every time I said good-bye, a small part of me wished I could stay.

AFTERWORD

For almost three years now, I'd been visiting the prison regularly, but I'd never been anywhere other than the school and the library, and I was curious to see the rest of the institution. I'd requested a tour from the warden, John Wolfe,* and in April 2015 he granted my request. In fact, he was kind enough to escort me around the prison himself, accompanied by a quiet and polite female CO named Officer Bell.

That morning, I saw all the places I'd heard the men talk about so often over the last two and a half years: the cellblocks with their double rows of tiers, the dining halls, the factories, and the hospital (although, perhaps understandably, I didn't get to see the lockup). As we walked across the compound, Wolfe,

---

*In February 2015, Stephen T. Moyer was appointed secretary of the Maryland DPSCS. In September 2015, he promoted Wolfe and replaced him with a new warden named Lyons. The Hobbesian undertones deserve note.

who's been warden of JCI for more than six years (the usual length of office is around four), elaborated on some of the many difficulties involved in running a maximum security prison, and I could see that he was proud of the facility's smoothly functioning operations. The three factories (the tag shop, the woodshop, and the sewing plant) were run with military precision, and the men who worked there appeared justly proud of their labor. In the woodshop we ran into Donald, leaning on his cane and taking a break with a group of his fellow workers, and in the sewing plant we ran into a surprised and sweaty Sig, who'd been crawling up in the loft, dusting away cobwebs in advance of an inspection. I was hoping he'd be impressed to see me in the warden's company, but when I saw him in the school later that day, he asked with mild curiosity, "Who was that old guy you were with?"

When we visited F building, the cellblock where the latest stabbing had taken place (an attack by the gang known as Dead Man Inc.), the warden invited me to observe the prisoners' living space. He pressed his face against the glass of a cell window and gestured that I should do the same. I did. It took a moment for my eyes to get accustomed to the darkness. Suddenly, inside the depths of the cell, there was a sudden movement, like that of an animal scuttling out of sight.

I immediately stepped back. I'd assumed I'd been brought to this block because the men were at lunch.

"There's someone in there," I said.

"It's all right. They're used to it," said the warden. "We do it all the time. That's how we take the count."

I couldn't put my face back against the glass. It felt so invasive. What if the man who lived there was on the toilet, or getting changed? The men's need for privacy might have explained why all the cells were dark. ("We're all like vampires in here" was Day-Day's reasoning, when I asked about it later.)

When we visited the prison hospital, we entered through the rear, behind one of the dining rooms. On the ground, next to a trash can, a robin was hopping along with an enormous cricket in its mouth. With each hop, the bird shifted the insect's twitching, writhing body a little farther down its throat. This sight, mixed with the smell of the trash and the heat, made me feel slightly nauseous.

We walked into the dark of the hospital and down a series of hallways with no exterior light, passing rooms with interior windows like the classrooms in the school, only smaller and more closely packed. There were waiting rooms lined with prisoners, cramped doctors' offices, a dentist's office, telehealth facilities, dialysis units, X-ray stations, climate-controlled rooms for isolating infected patients, psychologists' and social workers' offices, reception areas, and a group therapy room.

"This is the only part of the building left over from the 1950s," said Warden Wolfe as we passed through a sally port, inside which were plastic buckets placed on the ground to catch water from a leaky roof. "It's the only place where you'll actually see bars."

As he spoke, we arrived at a large, heavy iron gate manned by a CO who had the job of Cerberus, pulling open the heavy portal for those who were entering the underworld. We passed through the gate and entered a further network of dark hallways and waiting rooms known as the Regional Hospital, as it served other prisons in the local area. This part of the hospital—and the hospice that it contained—was truly grim. These wards, cut off from the daylight, contained dying men. A thin prisoner with a young, pale face and thick red beard lay on his bed turned toward me, pale and unseeing. A lone jogging shoe sat forlornly on a urine-stained pillow. Canned applause rang from a game show playing on the wall-mounted television.

Prisons are constructed for maximum surveillance and observation. In the dining halls, a row of upper-level windows ran the length of the room so the convicts could be scrutinized as they ate. There were also slots at intervals along the wall through which gas could be released in the event of a fight or a riot. In the workshops, after finishing their day's labor, men had to hang around until every single piece of equipment had been accounted for. This might seem understandable, but it's difficult to grasp just how much waiting is involved until you realize there are approximately four hundred men working in the factories, and most of them have to be strip-searched before leaving to ensure that they haven't concealed any glue, needles, or nails anywhere on their bodies.

What struck me above everything else, however, was the absolute barrenness of the place. Warden Wolfe mentioned budget cuts and the fact that we were at the tail end of the fiscal year, but I could tell this was more than a temporary austerity. It was, I realized, a large part of the desolation of prison life. Obviously, prisons aren't meant to be pretty, but as someone whose mood is attuned so closely to the aesthetics of my surroundings, I hadn't anticipated the cumulative depressing effect of lobbies, dining halls, corridors, and offices all completely void of decoration or color. Everything was minimal and functional. Outside of the library and school, I noticed no plants, rugs, cushions, posters, visual choices, or design features, just bare cinder-block walls, plain stainless steel tables, and cracked plastic chairs. Even in the offices of high-ranking prison authorities, dirty linoleum was peeling off the floors, and piles of ancient paperwork sat abandoned on filing cabinets that were rusting from damp. No wonder many of the people who worked here seemed unhappy and defensive. If I had to work in such a bleak environment, I thought, I'd probably be unhappy and defensive too.

The more time I spent at the prison, the more I began to question the assumptions I'd had going in. While on the one hand I'd always told myself that I could easily have ended up in the predicament of any of these fellow creatures—that there but for the grace of God go I—on the other hand, I knew I was fascinated and excited by the danger and strangeness of the place, by the rituals of culture and race that were inaccessible to me. I was drawn by the fact that these prisoners were my fellow human beings, and also by the fact that I'd never know others like them. Over time, however, what was once mysterious and alluring became difficult and confusing, and while I continued to sympathize instinctively with the men, their suffering began to exhaust me, and I realized that rather than learning more about them, I was simply learning how little I'm able to know.

I fell in love with literature because it offered me the chance to escape into a world that felt so much richer and deeper than the one I inhabited. I often thought that if I were ever unfortunate enough to find myself incarcerated, I'd be able to bear my situation as long as I had plenty of books to escape into. Now, however, I understand the misguided assumptions behind my fantasy—that the biggest difficulty for the prisoner is finding ways to pass the time. Contrary to popular assumptions, most prisoners aren't locked in their cells all day with nothing to do. They have a strict daily schedule, and when they are locked in their cells, they may not be able to read. Their cellmates may be watching television or playing a noisy video game. Or they may not have time to escape into books. This might be the only chance they get to work on their legal case, write letters, or catch up on their sleep.

My tour of JCI showed me that what the prison needed most urgently wasn't literature but all kinds of practical things: better medical facilities, more vocational opportunities for the prisoners, more showers, more telephones, better pay and training for COs, a functioning computer network, and for-credit college courses. Literature, I'm sure most of the men would agree, is not a necessity. In fact, if the prisoners had the option of better food at the cost of a smaller library, there's no question where the vote would come down.

At the prison, my relationships with the men grew closer as time passed, but this closeness emerged from our structured, predictable routine and defined boundaries. At the end of each session, the convicts went back to their cells, I drove home to Baltimore, and everything stayed as it was. It was a long time before I understood the importance of this stability, and it was brought home to me only when I encountered two of the prisoners in the outside world. This experience was both a shock and a revelation.

Oddly enough, when their release dates came up, not all men wanted to get out of prison. Some would mess up deliberately because they were afraid they wouldn't be able to support themselves on the outside. They often got into serious trouble right before they were due to be released, providing themselves with an apparently involuntary excuse for extending their prison terms. Authorities were aware that any improvements to prison life, such as allowing the men to have televisions in their cells or providing improvements in food, increased the chances of this happening. For someone like Vincent, who'd been in prison for most of his life, apprehension at the approach of his release date must have been especially intense. In the back of his mind must have been the fear that, upon being released, he'd discover he was no longer capable of living freely in polite society.

I was surprised how easily Vincent seemed to adjust to civilian life: he attributed the smoothness of his transition to all the time he'd spent at JCI in the school and the library, liaising between prisoners and outside guests. After his release, at age fifty-five, he moved in with his sister, who lived in a small bayside community just outside Baltimore, and began working for his brother-in-law's computer business. From prison, he'd been involved in various different campaigns to reduce violence and draw attention to victims' rights, and on the outside this commitment intensified. As a matter of course, his release had certain conditions attached. He had to wear an ankle monitor, meet with his probation officer twice a week, have his blood tested regularly, and keep to a 7:00 p.m.–to–7:00 a.m. curfew.

Meeting Vincent on the outside was a bizarre and amazing experience. It was as though he were a time traveler or an alien from another world. The simplest things were miraculous to him: cappuccinos, drinks in glass bottles, curly fries. He had to learn how to use e-mail and pump gas. I got a vicarious thrill out of just walking down the street with him, witnessing his pleasure as he greeted strangers. He loved being seen as just another passerby rather than as a dangerous criminal. I went with him to get measured for a suit, and he asked my advice on various color combinations, hoping to look dapper enough to impress a woman. I took him to the SPCA to look at strays that were up for adoption. Vincent was helping take care of his

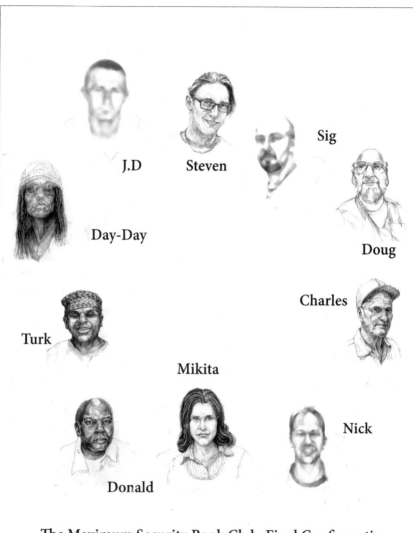

J.D   Steven   Sig

Day-Day   Doug

Charles

Turk

Mikita

Nick

Donald

The Maximum Security Book Club: Final Configuration

sister's dog, Scoobie, but he longed for a dog of his own; in fact, he wanted three. He'd run around the block with my dog, Oliver, at top speed. As soon as it was spring, I promised him, we'd take Oliver to the park and let him off the leash.

As soon as he got his own cell phone, Vincent would call me constantly. Very soon I had to let him know it was too much and I couldn't be interrupted so frequently at work. Then he worked out how to text. "I'm a free J-bird," he texted on the afternoon of Thanksgiving 2014, "cooking and eating a free range bird and listening to Freebird by Lynyrd Skynyrd THANKFUL for family, friends, and good food!" Later, when he discovered picture characters, his epic texts were punctuated with smiley faces, balloons, dolphins, dogs, and sunbursts.

Then one day, out of the blue, the epic texts stopped appearing.

Vincent was back in prison.

He'd been granted permission by his parole officer to go to a victims' rights event, which had then been rescheduled due to bad weather. He'd let his parole officer know about the change of plans, but either she hadn't gotten the message or had forgotten to make a note of it. Either way, his ankle monitor had sent out an alarm, and as far as the police were concerned, he'd broken his parole. He was returned not to JCI but to the Maryland Penitentiary right behind the notorious Baltimore City Detention Center, where he waited for his case to come up before the parole commissioner. Three weeks passed. A month. Two months. By the middle of March 2015, the long, harsh winter was finally coming to an end, but Vincent was still behind bars.

If things went badly, he wrote to me, he could be sent back to prison for seventeen years. It all depended on the commissioner.

"I am scared," he wrote. "Scared of what will happen to my

family but also really scared of what I may become if I don't get out."

All he could do was wait.

His parole hearing took place at the end of March, and to everyone's great relief he was released the same day. That weekend I visited him at his sister's home in Orchard Beach. He'd lost almost twenty pounds and looked terrible, but instead of feeling resentful at his rearrest, as I'd expected, he was full of relief and gratitude. We walked down to the bay with Oliver and Scoobie. The dogs ran and played in the water, and I took my shoes off and went in with them. Vincent couldn't join us: he couldn't get his ankle bracelet wet.

The first time he'd been released, he'd seemed to be heading in the right direction; now, however, he seemed depleted and bereft. At JCI, Vincent had been an important figure, a negotiator and a leader with a high level of responsibility. He'd been trusted by prison authorities and even had his own office desk piled high with papers. Perhaps this, I thought, was why I'd never noticed how small he was. Today, for the first time, I saw he was a diminutive figure, much shorter than me. His hair seemed to have turned thin and gray since I'd last seen him, and he had a determination to make up for lost time that was moving but, I felt, misguided.

He was on an eager quest to find a girlfriend. He hung out at the casino and spent a week alone in Ocean City. He continued to text me almost every day, but the things he invited me to do were the kinds of things that anyone who knew me well would never have suggested. I'd told him many times that I disliked crowds and needed the weekends to write. Still, the texts flooded in: "r you up for the aquarium, the science center?" "do u like comedy clubs, museums?" "what r u up to this weekend?" "want

STEVEN AND VINCENT, BALTIMORE HARBOR,
JULY 28, 2015

to go on a little cruz this weekend?" "want to see some live
music, blues?" "whats ur schedule this week? want to do nite life,
casino, etc?" "r u around tonite?" "want to go bowling?"

At one point I suggested to Vincent that, since he seemed to
want to see me so badly, we should start another book club along
with Steven, who'd also been released. I imagined the three of us
meeting at my house, to be joined by the other guys one by one
as those who were up for parole were gradually released. "OK"
texted Vincent, "but also some fun activities . . . ie hang out on
the beach go swimming casino etc." That put my ridiculous idea

in its place. The fact is, outside the book club, Vincent didn't want to discuss books. He was far more interested in talking about boats. He took to wearing a Greek fisherman's hat; he was planning to live on an old cabin cruiser he hoped to buy with the last of his savings, although at the time of writing he was still caught up in bureaucratic struggles involving inspection and insurance documents.

Meeting Steven on the outside almost broke my heart. I was forced to confront my projections and idealizations more directly than ever before, and the result was not pretty. From the way he'd expressed his passions in the book club, and from his constitutional optimism, I'd believed Steven to be a vigorous young thinker, a marvel of intuition and insight. He'd managed to maintain his natural buoyancy even in prison, I'd felt, and had emerged with ambition and the will to succeed. His, I thought, was the philosophy of the blue-eyed harlequin in *Heart of Darkness*: "when one is young one must see things, gather experience, ideas; enlarge the mind."

Thanks to the magic of "Go Home" Cardin, a hearing was held to reconsider Steven's sentence a year before he was even due for parole. This took place on June 24, 2015, in La Plata, Maryland, where Steven was originally sentenced, and I made the two-hour drive from Baltimore to be there at 9:00 in the morning to testify on his behalf. I was oddly affected by the fact that Steven had no friends or family members to support him; the only people there for him were his mentor, his mentor's wife, Cardin, and myself. Despite his prison muscles and tattoos, poor Steven, in his orange jumpsuit and restraints, seemed, like Bartleby, "absolutely alone in the universe." I was surprised and delighted when the judge, after hearing evidence of Steven's good behavior in prison and his mentor's willingness to provide him with a home and pay for him to attend college, decided to suspend the balance of his sentence and release him on the basis of time served. He was now under the supervision of his mentor, who lived in Columbia, Maryland.

The following week, Steven texted me. "Is there anyway you can come grab me from la plata? Last night didn't exactly go as I had planned." It turned out he'd taken a taxi from Columbia to La Plata (at a cost of almost two hundred dollars) hoping to spend the night with a girl he'd met on Facebook, but when they got back to her house, her father, taking one look at Steven with his half-shaved head and prison tattoos, had thrown him out. He'd then checked into a motel and had no way of getting back home.

It was a lot to ask, but it was a rainy day and I had nothing else to do; plus, it would give me two hours to talk to Steven on the drive back to Baltimore. I wanted to find out what it was like for him on the outside. I'd had more of a kinship with Steven than with Vincent, I thought, who'd always been more interested in politics than in literature. Steven, with his thick prison-issue glasses, had really been a reader. Take away his muscles and tattoos, I thought, and he was basically a nerd. He even read outside the book club. Now he was about to start college. I knew we'd have a lot to share.

It was almost 2:00 p.m. when I arrived at La Plata. Checkout time at Steven's motel was 11:00, so he'd been waiting for nearly three hours. I found him outside the Kentucky Fried Chicken, and, having spent all his money on the taxi from Columbia, the first thing he needed was for me to buy him a belt. He'd left his somewhere the night before—he and the girl had gone swim-

ming in a creek—and he was holding up his pants with one hand.
Then he needed to eat. Finally, we set off back to Baltimore.

"I'm sorry you had to wait around so long," I said. "I hope you
brought a book to read."

"Nope," he said casually. "I read so many books in prison,
now there's all this other stuff to catch up on." He pulled out the
brand-new iPhone 6 his mentor had bought him, and zipped his
thumb across the screen.

"Like what?" I asked him.

"Porn," he said, with a grin. "I can't believe it's free on the
Internet! I've been watching every kind of porn I can find."

I might as well have been driving with a stranger. "Outside"
Steven was definitely not a nerd. He was confident, self-assured,
and preoccupied, constantly glancing at his phone. In a week
he'd already become uncannily proficient in the use of social
media. The energy I'd enjoyed so much in the book club had
found a new outlet, and rather than being "all alone in the universe," Steven already had over two hundred Facebook friends
and was juggling a number of different female admirers. As the
rain beat against the windshield, he talked idly about strippers,
webcams, and "this chick" he'd taken the two-hour taxi ride to
see. She was already "head over heels," he said, and he was thinking about asking her to be his girlfriend, although he didn't believe in monogamy.

That was July 2. Each time I saw him after that, I struggled to
find the Steven of the book club in this unfamiliar and arrogant
young man. He texted me only when he needed a ride or a loan.
He never e-mailed, he explained, because he was never home at
his computer (his living situation was complicated), and he could
only use the text and call functions on his phone because he used
up his data so quickly ("I exceed really fast"). When, after de-

scending to the level of what felt like undignified nagging—perhaps begging would be a better word—I finally got an e-mail out of him, it was not auspicious. "Really a lot of things that people think are important to me are not," he wrote. "Even though right now I am following the academic path I don't think that it is going to be one I pursue for long." This was August 4, 2015, three weeks before he was due to begin community college, six weeks after his release from prison. At the time of writing, Steven had begun attending his college classes, though a lot of things were still up in the air: whether he would continue to live with his mentor; whether he would stay in college full-time; whether we would stay in touch. He got distracted so easily that I sometimes wondered whether he would end up in prison again. But whenever I recalled his lonely, manacled figure in the courtroom, I thought again of the narrator's lines in "Bartleby"—"To a sensitive being, pity is not seldom pain. And when at last it is perceived that such pity cannot lead to effectual succor, common sense bids the soul rid of it."

Facing up to it, however, the sadness I felt was self-pity. There was no need for me to pity Steven. No question: both he and Vincent were incomparably happier and better off than their incarcerated shadow selves—the two men who'd talked to me so eloquently over the last three years about Bartleby and Macbeth, Mr. Kurtz and Dr. Jekyll. The book club, I realized now, existed only in my presence—to some degree only in my head, and in these pages—and in this sense it had always been an illusion. My Vincent and my Steven existed only in a certain time and space. They were phantoms that disappeared upon exposure to daylight. These two men, so alluring and charismatic in the prison, seemed, on their release, to emerge into the outside world like passengers climbing the steps out of the subway. As they gradually ascended into the daylight world, as my projections began to fade, Vincent and Steven seemed to turn into smaller, lesser, more ordinary versions of themselves, eventually becoming indistinguishable from other people, vanishing into the crowd. Once back amidst the practical concerns of daily life, neither had the slightest interest in reading or talking about books. This, I now knew, would be equally true for all the men who were released. I was not turning them into readers. They were just men who attended the prison book club. For me, it was as though a magic spell had been broken. On the inside, I'd loved those men. But on the outside, I'd lost them.

Because literature was all I had.

ACKNOWLEDGMENTS

The reading group at Jessup Correctional Institution is part of the JCI Prison Scholars Program, founded by Dr. Drew Leder of Loyola University in Baltimore. The JCI Prison Scholars program exists thanks to the support and assistance of Warden John Wolfe, librarian Grace Schroeder, Sergeant Sonji Lynn, and Security Chief Allen Gang. Thanks to my smart and energetic intern Shelby Norton, to Dr. Kevin McCamant for his insights about the workings of the prison, and to Gerard Shields at the Maryland Department of Public Safety and Correctional Services for his valuable support and assistance. Thanks to all my students and colleagues at the Maryland Institute College of Art, especially Stephen Towns for helping to coordinate the class I taught at JCI. Thanks also to those friends who came into the prison with me to share their talents with the men. Melissa Daum taught yoga sessions; Laura Wexler read from and discussed *Fire in a Canebrake*; Jess Bither joined the book club for a week; Jess Bastidas sketched portraits; and Mark Hejnar took photographs. I was impressed by the commitment and dedication shown by Baynard Woods during his visit to JCI and his conversations with the prisoners. His article about the prison college program, "Heart of Darkness," was published in the *Baltimore City Paper* on April 30, 2014.

To the Owl Bar writing group—John Barry, Paul Jaskunas, and Saul Myers—anticipation of your scrutiny always keeps me on my toes. You are my first and most discriminating readers. Thomas Jones gave me enormously helpful feedback on individual chapters of an earlier incarnation of this manuscript and made incomparable edits. I am hugely grateful to my brilliant agent Betsy Lerner, and to Terry Karten, my gracious editor at HarperCollins, and to everyone else who worked on this book, especially Jillian Verillo, Jarrod Taylor, and David Chesanow. Finally, David Sterritt supports all my endeavors, however unpleasant or unusual, without question or comment, which is one of the many reasons why I love him.

Most of all, this book would not have been possible without the collaboration of the incarcerated citizens of Jessup Correctional Institution in Maryland. It is dedicated, with deep gratitude and affection, to: Sig, Donald, Day-Day, Turk, Steven, J.D., Nick, Charles, Doug, Shaka, Ren, Vincent, Kevin, Alfie, and Guy.

Grateful acknowledgment is made for permission to reprint illustrations on the following pages:

xvii   Photo of Vincent by Bill Hughes.
4   Illustration of book club by Jess Bastidas.
9   Photo of Steven courtesy of Jessup Correctional Institution.
37   Illustration of Kevin by Jess Bastidas.
60   Photo of Charles courtesy of Jessup Correctional Institution.
72   Illustration of Guy by Jess Bastidas.
75   Photo of J.D. and Luke by Mark Hejnar.
94   Photo of Turk by Mark Hejnar.
98   Photo of Sig by Mark Hejnar.
119   Photo of Donald and Day-Day by Mark Hejnar.
130   Photo of Nick by Mark Hejnar.
156   Photo of Donald by Mark Hejnar.
192   Photo of Doug and Mikita by Mark Hejnar.
220   Illustration of book club by Jess Bastidas.

ABOUT THE AUTHOR

MIKITA BROTTMAN, PhD, is an Oxford-educated scholar, author, and psychoanalyst. She has written seven previous books, including *The Great Grisby: Two Thousand Years of Literary, Royal, Philosophical, and Artistic Dog Lovers and Their Exceptional Animals*, and is a professor of humanities at the Maryland Institute College of Art in Baltimore. She lives in Baltimore, Maryland, and continues with her weekly reading group at Jessup Correctional Institution.